To Emma.

Thank you fo " :)
my book promotion! I hope
you enjoy your reading!

Jon and Harry's
Year of Microadventure

best wishes.

Jon Doolan

This book is for Harry and Alastair – two inspirational dudes in their own rights.

Foreword

"I spent a decade chasing big adventures round the world. I have visited about 90 countries, and done expeditions in conditions varying from oceans to deserts to icecaps. Therefore, when I switched to embracing far briefer adventures close to home - microadventures - it felt like quite a culture shock. However, I began discovering the hidden wild spots of my own country and reaping the benefits of squeezing intermittent nights under the stars into the busy rush of normal life. Little by little, I became hooked on microadventures. The buzz of finding beautiful pockets of wilderness close to a big city. The peace and quiet of looking down at busy streets from my cozy hilltop bivvy bag. And the laughter and memories of sharing these little experiences with my friends. And so I began to evangelise about microadventures. I blogged about them and started encouraging others to give it a try. I wasn't sure if anyone would agree with me, or if the whole idea was just a bit ludicrous.

So I can't tell you how chuffed I was one evening, on the train home from giving a talk, when I unwrapped a gift copy of Jon's book. Reading the amusing highs and lows of a year of microadventures was an absolute delight. It is a story of adventure at the margins of busy normal life. It's also a story of two good friends spending time together and making many funny memories for themselves. I sincerely hope that it encourages some other people to buy a bivvy bag and give microadventures a try."

Alastair Humphreys

Prologue

It was while absentmindedly strolling through Waterstones pushing the baby buggy that I happened to pick up his book.

I say absentmindedly but my mind was actually feverish with the really important life questions, like how are hand-cooked crisps made? Which poor sod has to hold each individual slither of potato in the boiling hot fat? It must take an awful lot of factory workers standing over vats of molten cooking oil to make one bag of Kettle chips. Makes you appreciate each crunchy bite just that little bit more.

My wife, Sally, was off doing some serious Christmas shopping while I had been left to my own devices with the sleeping baby. I was dreaming of my life before my daughter came along. A life that through rose tinted glasses had seemed full of vigour and excitement. Now my brain-dead, sleep deprived, zombification had driven me to be like all the other mindless consumerist drones pushing a slumbering infant around retail stores.

Maybe the book had drawn me to it. Maybe it was the exciting cover picture of a man's face half submerged in dirty river water. Maybe it was the intriguing text where the unusual word 'MICROADVENTURE' had been split into three. Whatever it was that drew me to the book, draw me it did and there I was thumbing through the crisp pages.

By the end of the introduction I was intrigued. Here was a manual, a guide, on how to squeeze adventure into the busy schedule of everyday life. Here was inspiration to get adventure back into my life and still fulfil my commitments as a father and husband. Here was my ticket out of zombieland. I could shoehorn adventure into all the gaps between my normal everyday life. I could have my cake and eat it.

'Jon?' I could hear Sally calling. I put the book back on the shelf and I drove the pram out of the shop. In three steps my cerebral cortex had already forgotten about the book, one of many that I had picked up that day, that week, that festive month. As soon as the spark of inspiration had been ignited it was quickly extinguished by the onrushing importance of the impending festivities and the stress of the lack of presents currently purchased.

Maybe a nugget of burning ember was left behind.

A week passed and the usual mad rush to get the Christmas shopping ensued. The intensity of the almost daily incursions into retail hell continued well into the month with the constant balance of trying to buy thoughtful gifts with the ever present reasonably priced tat on every shelf beckoning for the easy bargain.

It's at times like these that you realise just how little you know about the interests of your family. My family is not particularly close with siblings spread throughout the country. However, increasingly, I have found that getting that thoughtful present is more easily done online. It avoids the scrum in the shopping aisles and enables you to handpick the relevant gifts. It allows you the peace of your own living room to make informed choices while consulting the various texts that you have received back from different members of the family. It does unfortunately mean that you need a modicum of organisation in your life, which I too often lack. Thankfully I have a wonderful wife who will do all this, send out the relevant cards to distant aunties and long lost cousins and arrange the correct gift for my nephew and niece each year. I am in charge of the wrapping though!

It was during one of these wrapping sessions that Sally's phone buzzed. She briefly glanced at it before handing me the next gift that was to be wrapped in pointlessly expensive landfill filler.

Seriously, what is the point in wrapping paper? It costs a ridiculous amount of money for what boils down to a colourful piece of litter. With my mild form of OCD it takes an age to wrap each individual item. It is torn in seconds from the gift that has been so lovingly wrapped. It is screwed up and bundled into a big black bag and is hopefully shoved in the recycling. Why not skip out the middle man and just hand presents to people in plastic bags. At least, in this new enlightened eco-conscious era, the packaging will save the gift receiver 5p at Morrisons.

Sally relayed the message in the text she had just received. 'Mum wants to know what you want for Christmas,' she said looking up to me expectantly.

Now this is a difficult situation which I have evolved a solution to. The worst response is: 'Tell you're mum not to worry about it. I don't need anything from her this year.' Uh err! Wrong answer! This is definitely not what the mother-in-law wants to hear. If

I say that I don't want anything she will take this as a clear indication that 1) I am an imbecile who can't even make a decision. What on earth am I doing being married her daughter and 2) Oh, well. I may as well get him that disgusting woolly jumper from the charity shop that I bought on a whim and can't think who to give it to. No, no. Also a bad response would be: 'Tell her I don't mind what she gets me.' The rest of the Christmas period would be spent scratching the wool rash that is developing around my neck. Best option – ask for a book.

A book? Yes, a book. You don't have to wear it. You don't have to be seen with it in public. You don't have to interact with it for the entire Christmas holidays. After which, mother-in-law would have already forgotten what she got you for Christmas. Unless it's something that is life changing (the Koran for instance) you can expect your lifestyle to stay pretty much the same as well. And as long as you avoid erotic fiction and Mein Kampf, a book is the perfect present from a mother-in-law.

'A book!' I said brightly.

'Which book?' Sally was now looking at me exasperatedly, letting her mobile dangle from her hand like the response to her mother was our greatest priority right now, despite the ever-present pile of unwrapped gifts she was sitting in front of.

Which book to choose? There are literally thousands of books out there (probably more!). What was that book I saw in Waterstones just the other day? Micro-something or other. An ember in my brain started to glow. That's it.

'Microadventures book,' I smiled across to Sally waving a roll of Celotape triumphantly.

'Whatever,' she said as she typed the mysterious word into the phone and tapped SEND.

The ember grew brighter.

So again I forgot about the book. In the hurly-burly of Christmas everything just seems to go in a blur of tinsel and stuffing. The festivities were the usual excitement but with the extra special addition of our little girl who was enjoying her second Christmas but the first one where she might have some inkling of what is going on. It was also the first Christmas that we had spent at home rather than at the in-laws. It was splendid having the late night preparations. The traditions that my wife and I both bring to the melting pot of our family. The new traditions that we make together. Getting ready for Father Christmas.

Being woken by Rosie's cries while still lying in my own bed on a beautiful crisp Christmas morning. The confused excitement at finding a stocking full of toys, sweets and the obligatory satsuma at the bottom of the bed. The joy of seeing her eyes light up as she saw the mountain of presents under the tree that she could start ripping the wrapping paper off (Grrr!).

The mid-morning mad dash around the M25 to get to the in-laws for Christmas lunch (with extra Brussel sprouts just for me!) before collapsing on the sofa in front of an old movie or new comedian.

Total Christmas bliss.

'Did you get your present?' Sally's mum, Maíre, asked sweetly.

'Yep, thanks Maíre. I'll be reading that later. Probably.' I said popping another Cadbury's Milk Tray into my overstuffed gob. I was sat surrounded by my various gifts indulging in some after dinner decadence. The Great Escape was reaching its usual conclusion on the TV. I patted the book that was on the arm of the chair, effectively giving the man on the front cover an affectionate slap in the face. I looked down again at the cover, at the twinkling eyes of the man, who I assumed was the author, Alastair Humphreys. I picked up the book and began to thumb the pages again.

I didn't put it down.

The ember burst into flames.

'Buy this! I've just got one. Plans for adventure and fun are afoot!!' read the text that I sent my best mate, Harry, on Boxing Day. I also sent a link to Alpkits Hunka bivvy bag.

'Will do!' came the reply.

'If you don't get 1 you won't get your Xmas present!'

'I'll order it now'

I'd read the 'Microadventures' book front to back and back to front in less than an afternoon. I'd read so many of Alastair Humphreys blog posts that it felt like my eyes were bleeding. I'd even ordered a copy to arrive on Harry's doorstep by the first of January.

To say I was inspired was like saying New Year's Eve is always an anti-climax. Dead-right on both accounts.

January

On top of everything else, Harry split up with his girlfriend of one year. She was working in Jersey while he was stuck in a rut in Leighton Buzzard just outside of London. Bad times.

'Hey H, how's the flat viewing going?' I asked when I called him shortly after finding out.

'It's a bugger. Looked around a whole load of crap places. Got one lined up though so I should be out of her flat in the next week or so.'

'Ah, that's good. Listen, if you want to take your mind off things, you're more than welcome to come and visit if you fancy it.'

'I might just do that. What about Saturday?'

'Saturday's good. Let me just check with Sally… She says that's fine. Get here in the morning and we can go and get some kit.'

'What kit?'

'You'll see!'

'Ooo! This is exciting!'

'This is a great idea! I've always wanted to go to a GoOutdoors!' Harry exclaimed as we wandered through the warehouse. The shelves teemed with cut price fleeces and multi-coloured sleeping bags dangled from the rafters.

'So, you didn't order the bivvy?'

'No.'

'That's typical you, that is!'

'I'm sure they'll have one in here.'

They didn't. We traipsed round GoOutdoors for an hour, pestering shop assistants and dismantling displays looking for the elusive piece of kit. GoOutdoors is like a gentleman's club. If you are a member you get massive discounts on a lot of the stock, which I assume is what happens in those exclusive establishments. Like a Makro or Costco but for hill walkers and campers rather than dodgy kebab vans and corner shops. I can't shake the feeling that the prices that are offered to the members are in fact the normal prices and the 'non-member' prices are just mentally expensive. You'd have to be a complete moron to shop there without a card. But you have to be pretty savvy to spot the actual bargains mixed in with the standard price waterproof jackets and enormous tents. It's all a very clever marketing con.

Another way that GoOutdoors likes to make you part with your cash is showing you all the products as they would be if you were using them. From small camp stoves that have been ready set up, to sleeping bags that hung out so you can see the size. From display cabinets with Swiss army knives with every appendage on show to full blown ten man tents erected for your perusal. There is one area that baffles me though. How can walking over a small wooden bridge possibly equate to hiking a mountain in a snazzy pair of walking boots? That little brown incline in the shoe and boot section of the shop is pretty much useless. Tell a lie. It has one function. It keeps small children occupied as they clamber up and down its worn surface like a mini climbing frame.

'Mate, we've looked for ages, and Rosie is starting to get bored of that wooden bridge thing in the shoe section. I don't think we're going to find a bivvy.'

'I've found something even better.' Harry held aloft a small black bag.

'What is it?'

'It's a hammock.'

'Is it going to work?'

'Dunno.'

'Is it even waterproof?'

'Dunno.'

'Brilliant. Where's Rosie?'

'Dunno.'

'Bollocks!'

We found my daughter jumping up and down on a blow up mattress in a huge tent and took our small pile to the till, paid and left.

'I've read that you should have a big dinner before going on one of these microadventures,' I told Harry when we got back to the house, 'So I've put a lamb stew in the slow-cooker and we can have that later.'

'Look at you with your slow-cooker. You're such an old git.'

'One of Sally's Christmas presents. She's going back to work in February and this is meant to make our lives easier. Apparently.'

'Right, what should we do now then?' Harry's question had me a bit stumped. This was going to be our first microadventure so I'd thought of something small. There is a park nearby that I thought might be a good place to set up a wild camp. Not too far from home that if it did become unbearable then we could just come home but a little bit more distant than my back garden. I hadn't planned a big trek or a complicated journey or anything. I just wanted to see if this microadventure thing was as fun and exciting as I thought it might be.

'I don't think we want to go and make our camp before it gets dark.' I said, pondering. I didn't fancy being accosted by landowners or aggravated by aggressive teenagers who might happen to be frequenting the park at this early hour. I suggested a venue that would mean we could sit in warmth and comfort as we waited for the sun to go down. There'd be food and drink available, the low hubbub of a crowd of people to disquiet my and Harry's nervous fears and they've even got a fruit machine. 'Pub?'

'Yes!'

It was January so the sun went down quite early in the evening. We were sat in the Harvest Moon at 4pm thinking about our rumbly tummys and the lamb hotpot that was bubbling away back home that wouldn't be ready for hours. We could see out the window the sun dipping below the treetops and we were itching to head out before the twilight disappeared.

'Let's just get a quick bite here and we can have the lamb stew tomorrow,' I said.

'Do you think that's a good idea? Shouldn't you be having a big dinner before you go on this micro-whatever it is?' asked Sally as she turned to remove the table fork from Rosie's vice like grip.

'No, we'll be fine.' I said supping my pint.

'I can't wait!' Harry said reaching for the menu a massive grin plastered across his grizzly chops. 'This is going to be AWESOME!' He pushed his glasses up his nose as he read from the menu.

I knew Harry would be the perfect person to bring on this adventure with me. He is just a manic bag of energy, full of enthusiasm for literally anything and loves doing something a little bit different. He has crazy dark hair which is streaked with a white slash like he suffered a serious electric shock as a child. His artfully dishevelled look has taken years of mastering and an expense he refuses to share with me. His wild hair style, his thick rimmed glasses and his permanent maniacal grin make him look like a mad scientist. To be honest, he quite literally IS a mad scientist. He creates insane food contraptions for a living. Like the jelly-bean-fountain, the liquid-nitrogen-ice-cream machine and the chicken-soup-washing-machine machine. He is a proper lunatic and makes money from it. I'm not jealous in the slightest!

We were well stuffed with bog-standard pub grub. By bog-standard I don't mean that it tasted like a bog or was cooked in the bog. 'Bog-standard' is an odd phrase, isn't it? I don't think bogs are particularly standard. I've been in some absolute s-holes and I've been in some immaculate lavatories. I wonder where 'bog-standard' comes from? Nevermind. I'm being sidetracked.

We left the Harvest Moon and waved goodbye to Sally and the sprog. Sally had kindly offered to do the bedtime routine that evening which meant I was free. What is the first thing most blokes do when they have a free evening? That's right. Booze!

Sainsbury's was little more than 20 steps away from the front door of the pub. We made a bee-line for the alcohol aisle. And by bee-line I mean we went straight there, not buzzed back and forth like a bee. Don't get me started.

'Have you ever tried sloe gin?' Harry asked.

'No. It's a bit of an old man's drink, isn't it?'

'Nah, it's a real man's drink.'

He grabbed a bottle of Gordon's from the shelf and we made our way to the till. The perplexed cashier did not know what to think of two lads dressed in about thirty layers between them one of them with a GoPro attached to a cycling helmet attached to his head. With our bottle of sloe gin we looked like a couple of mentally challenged alcoholic tramps splashing out on some decent booze. I felt that a bottle of White Lightning or a four pack of Special Brew would have suited out look better.

'Are you two going camping tonight?' she asked eyeing up our sleeping bags that we had tucked under our arms.

'You could say that,' smiled Harry as he punched the digits on the card machine.

'It's a bit cold, isn't it?' she asked.

'Yep, it's going to be zero degrees tonight.' I replied grinning inanely.

'That's why we look like fat eskimos,' Harry added. He was right. We had studied the BBC weather app on our phones before we'd left to go to the pub earlier. As a result we had plastered ourselves in as many pieces of clothing we could wear while still being able to bend our joints. I personally had ten layers on top. TEN! I know! That's not even an exaggeration. I counted. I think I may have overdone it. In the pub it had felt extreme. Even now, stood at the till in Sainsbury's I had a gentle sheen on my forehead.

'While we're here, do we need anything else?' Harry asked as we walked through the sliding doors into the chill night air.

'We've got booze. What more do we need?'

'Then let's go!'

We were like two kids on Christmas Eve excited about the presents we were going to get the next morning. The only thing I would be unwrapping, however, was my own exhausted body out of the sleeping bag. We were giddy with the thrill of camping out wild, doing something that maybe we shouldn't have been. It was like the feeling when you were a kid when you made a den in your back garden or even a house using the cushions from the sofa. You would love to have spent the whole night out there in your rough stick lean to or under your collapsible cushion construction but you knew at some point your mum would be calling you and you'd have to go and get into your pyjamas and climb into your own safe bed.

We're grownups and we don't have to listen to our mums any more. Tonight Harry and I would be defying that safe bed. We were going to make a den and stay in it all night. We were going to sleep in our everyday clothes. We weren't even going to brush our teeth! We were sticking up for that young version of ourselves who resented the call to normality and the safe comfort of a duvet and warm cosy bed...

with soft pillows...

and central heating...

in January when it was going to be zero degrees.

Oh God! What on earth were we doing?!

We headed to the edge of town where there was a big open field in a park. Because Harry didn't have a bivvy or roll mat and only had a hammock we needed to find some trees. Unfortunately, those around the perimeter of the park were thin whippets of trees that wouldn't have supported an Action Man toy let allowed a mop-haired gangly moron like Harry. We walked a bit further, crossed a bridge over the ring road and headed off down a country footpath.

Going beyond the ring road was a big step. We were properly out of town now. The street lights were behind us and we were off into the wilderness… of the Hertfordshire countryside!

We didn't go far though. After a short walk we found a copse near a stream by a field that had trees that would support H's weight. With feverish excitement we set up camp next to the gently gurgling water in the middle of the small copse. When you have a hammock, a bivvy and a roll mat, it takes almost no time at all so we cracked the seal on the bottle of gin and started glugging back the warming purple liquid.

It was then that we noticed that we'd clearly set up our camp over the top of some sort of animal route to get down to the stream. We debated the merits of Harry being woken in the middle of the night by a badger nosing his butt as he swung in the hammock above the animal track but in the end we couldn't be bothered to move the camp.

We left the camp where it was and climbed back out through the foliage to the field. The clouds had moved and we realised that we could see perfectly clearly by the light of the full moon and didn't need our head torches, so turned them off. Taking turns glugging from the liquor bottle we went for a long walk discussing all things trivial and important. Harry told me about his difficult break up with his ex-girlfriend and his endeavours on Tinder to find a replacement. I told him about my difficulties balancing my selfish activities with my commitments as a father and husband. We had one of those chats that you only really have with your best mate when you have some alone time together and both of you are getting pretty smashed. It'd been far too long since we'd had a proper heart to heart and a real male bonding session. The joint nervous anticipation of spending a night outside under the stars for the first time made us closer and the sloe gin made our tongues looser. It was a really lovely, almost romantic, night walking under the full moon gazing up at the majesty of the Milky Way as we discussed our inner frailties and concerns with each other.

Oh dear. This story has taken a weird turn. It's all gone a bit Brokeback Mountain there. I feel like I should write that we were holding hands and shared a kiss in the moonlight. We didn't.

Erm. Let's get this back on track.

So we went for a walk. We came back to the camp. We climbed into our respective beds (separately!). Harry clambered into his hammock while trying to not let his trainers which had accumulated about half a field of clay on the bottom touch any of his sleeping apparatus. It was quite entertaining. Eventually, finally, we both just lay there and stared up at the moon. Its amazing brightness peeking out between the bare boughs of the trees and it bathed the whole area in a spooky patchwork of deep dark shadows and bright white clarity. It was a beautiful evening.

After about thirty seconds of being stuffed into my cocoon of a bivvy I had to explode out of it. I was burning up. Clearly wearing ten top layers in a three season sleeping bag, no matter what the temperature outside, was overkill. I stripped off three layers and stuffed them to the bottom of my bag to keep them warm for later should I need them. I gave my mini pillow a fluff and then snuggled back in to sleep.

By the way, I'm assuming that you know what a bivvy is, but maybe you don't, so I better explain. A bivvy is like a rain coat for your sleeping bag. Other people have described it variously as a campers condom, the human slug and badger bait. It is basically a waterproof layer that goes around your sleeping bag that means that you can sleep outdoors without the need for a tent. You still need a roll mat to insulate you from the cold floor but essentially all your camping gear can fit into a small rucksack. It is actually amazing. You should definitely try it. If by the end of this story you are not convinced then I have absolutely failed to inspire you in how amazing wild camping with a bivvy is.

Speaking of the story, I seemed to have got side-tracked again. I was just talking about how I had such an amazing sleep, which bearing in mind I was lying on the floor in a small wood is pretty impressive. I was awoken at about 3am when the local boy racers decided to use the patch of ring road that was adjacent to our field as a drag racing strip. This was nothing compared to the many hours sleep

I have lost at home due to having a small girl that needs perpetual midnight attention. I soon was unconscious again.

When finally my eyelids creaked open the weak early morning sun was valiantly trying to battle through a sea of fog and failing miserably. It felt eerie waking up in the woods with the ceaseless tinkling stream still dripping away in the gloom. The dark shape of Harry's hammock hung motionless a metre or so away and I daren't move a muscle.

Mr. Hangover decided that it wasn't going to pity the poor father of one who rarely drinks and hadn't had a night out in months. Instead, Mr. Hangover decided that now was the best time to do some serious demolition work on the inside of my skull. He had gotten together all of his loudest and most violent tools and was currently repeatedly bringing a sledgehammer down on the back of my eyeballs.

I'm sure I let out a small groan because it was at that moment that Harry shuffled in his hammock and gave a moan of his own. I tried to call out to him but it seems Mr. Hangover had decided to turn off the mains water before he started on his DIY because my throat was as dry as sandpaper.

'Urgh!' moaned Harry as he shuffled into a position where he could see me. 'How did you sleep mate?'

Eventually I produced enough saliva to enable speech. 'Yeah, great. Apart from those tossers driving like idiots at three this morning.' I coughed hoarsely. 'Do we have any water?'

'We have more gin,' said Harry pointing at the three quarters empty bottle that was balanced on a rotten log nearby. Bile rose in my gullet as I eyed the evil liquid.

'Didn't we get any water from Sainsbury's last night?'

'No. You said we didn't need anything else.'

'Oh.' I sat up despite my aching body protesting. I was like a zombie caterpillar rising from a coffin. Mr. Hangover decided to take a pick axe to the back of my head and I swayed visibly. 'I don't feel great.'

'You don't look great.'

'You don't look too great either. How did you sleep?'

'Yeah fine, apart from I froze my butt off. I had to keep rolling over to make sure my bum wasn't always at the bottom of the hammock and getting all the wind chill. But every time I rolled over all the iced condensation that was inside my hammock fell in my face. All in all, I had a brilliant night's sleep.'

'Should've bought a bivvy then.'

'Yeah, yeah.'

Bit by bit we both extracted ourselves from our sleeping arrangements and started to take apart our small camp. The worst bit was having to slide our feet into our freezing clay sodden shoes. I had to leave Harry to it at one stage as Mr. Hangover was using a pneumatic drill on my medulla oblongata and all body functions were in danger of ceasing. We scrambled out of the woods and gazed around ourselves in the frosty field. There wasn't a lot of gazing happening because fog had fallen like a curtain and we could only see about twenty paces in any direction. Crunching along the icy footpath we had used the night before we made our way back over the bridge over the ring road and back to civilisation.

And reheated lamb stew.

So I found an email for the local newspaper. The Herts and Essex Observer. A news reporter got back to me. I sent a link of our video of our first microadventure and then I forgot about it.

Harry had obviously been bitten by the microadventure bug. Two weeks later he broke all of the unspoken rules in our mini microadventure team. He messaged me a link to a youtube video. I clicked on it. It was him.

He'd only gone and bloody done a microadventure without me. On his own. Loser!

To be fair to him he had invited me but I had already committed myself to something else. At this stage I really can't remember what it was. It was obviously not as exciting as Harry's solo effort looked.

The video was pretty well edited with Harry pootling around some country roads on his push bike with a backpack obviously crammed with camping gear and extra layers. The highlight of the vid was when he got lost. He found an old pile of straw that looked ideal to bivvy in. He also found a family of field mice getting mightly miffed that he was using their house as a mattress.

I was obviously gutted that I'd missed out on his microadventure. Particularly as it had taken place in the middle of the day on a weekend. This was a massive benefit as you could actually see what he was doing rather than pitch blackness which was the mainstay of our previous adventure (and many adventures to come). The spontaneity of just getting up on a Saturday morning and thinking 'You know what, I'm just going to go for a cycle somewhere and camp wherever I feel like,' is fabulous. The pure, utter freedom of it. And it's not even difficult. Life sometimes really just gets in the way of adventure. I was extremely envious of Harry. What a tosser!

February

About three years ago, I (or rather a friend of ours – long story!) had challenged us to take a swim outdoors in winter. Harry had ended up taking a dip off of his house boat into the Thames. I'd run into the Solent near Portsmouth in my pants. Needless to say neither of them was very dramatic.

What I'd really wanted to do was swim in the Serpentine. More specifically I'd wanted to join the Serpentine Swimming Club, grease myself up in goose fat on Christmas morning and dive into sub-zero water like Victorian gentleman of old. The website with its health and safety disclaimers and waiver forms that needed signing and warnings of putrid diseases just made it all the more enticing. However, that had been three years ago and my quest for Serpentine submersion had been about as successful as a squirrel winning the next summer Olympics 100m freestyle.

In our new bible, Microadventures, Alastair has lauded the joy and wonders and benefits of outdoors swimming and he tries to do it on every microadventure that he can. He also encourages you to squeeze your adventures into the middle of the week deeming that a school night is just as useful as any for a microadventure. Lastly, in the said hallowed tome, Al points out that it doesn't really matter what you do on a microadventure and there is no such thing a failing a microadventure. Just getting out the house and doing something that you wouldn't normally do is enough to make it adventurous.

Obviously, all of this is a massive cop out. Basically, I just really wanted to swim in the Serpentine.

Even the name sounds mysterious, like something out of Harry Potter or something. I half expected to look at a map and see a snake's head at one end of the river. Alas, there was no forked tongue or hypnotic eyes. To be honest it looks more like a skinny whale. I did establish that the river ran through Hyde Park in London and that the nearest tube was Hyde Park Corner, so it was here that I agreed to meet Harry one afternoon after work.

In the olden days, when Harry lived and worked in London, an after work meet would have been relatively easy. As it was Harry had to travel all the way in from Leighton Buzzard on the train while I had to travel across from Essex on the tube. We didn't end up meeting until about 8pm by which time it had been dark for hours. Typical.

I arrived early and wandered aimlessly into Hyde Park. The contrast between the relative tranquillity of the park and the noise blaring of taxi horns and the hubbub of people who still milled about on Knightsbridge was quite remarkable. Just a few short strides into the park and the relative peace and tranquillity descends like a smothering blanket.

You also notice as you look up that all but the brightest stars are invisible in central London and like absent friends I lamented their loss. The light pollution is just too strong in the city and as much as the stars like to twinkle, twinkle, they can't compete with the electric glow of the street lamps. Not that this would have mattered anyway. Dense cloud cover obscured the entire night sky.

I was amazed at how much my senses were heightened in the park. Maybe it was the river itself. The sound of one of those drill sergeant style fitness groups finished off some gruelling exercises bounced across from the other side of the water. Maybe it was the sharp contrast between the incessant noise of the city and the calm quiet of the park. Maybe it was the adrenaline of my 'fight or flight' reflexes as I was sure I was going to be mugged at any moment. Maybe it wasn't quite that tranquil after all.

Harry arrived at the allotted time (which is actually a small miracle in itself) and I met him at the underground gates. We embraced in manly fashion before we exited the station. As we were walking out about a dozen lightly dressed runners bundled through the subway and out a different exit in a bewildering flash of colourful Lycra and running vests. The Serpentine Running Club was out in full force this evening which made me think again about the Serpentine Swimming Club that I'd been so desperate to join.

While we're at the tube, can I point out something that really puzzles me? No? I'm doing it any way. Imagine you are driving down the road. Imagine there is a car in front of you. Which side of the car do you pass on? If you said right then you are probably in the UK. If you said left, then you are driving in one of the many countries of the world who drive on the right (and overtake on the left). You're also doing it all wrong, by the way, but I'll let you off.

Ok, so in England we overtake on the right because we drive on the left. Why on earth then when you visit the iconic London

Underground, a world renowned, legendary, historic landmark, why, oh why, do we insist that everyone 'stands' on the right and 'overtakes' on the left. It's absolutely bizarre that we can get our road systems so right but then cock it up so royally on escalators in the tube. It's far too European for my liking.

Anyway, Harry and I made our way out to the park, dodging cyclists who despite the darkness had outright refused to install lights on their bikes. We found ourselves staring out over the black water of the Serpentine in minutes. The flat inky black surface reflected the lights from the buildings and street lamps on the far side of river perfectly. The cold air was still.

We walked along the path that ran along the water's edge until we were far enough away from that dodgy couple who were still feeding the ducks and swans at this ungodly hour.

Harry looked at me. I looked at Harry. We both looked at the huge sign that read:

No Bathing
No Bathing, fishing or dogs allowed in this lake.
Thank you for your cooperation.

'Look Jon, you can't go swimming here. It says 'no dogs'.'

'Ha, ha. You're hilarious. Seriously though. Do you think we might get in trouble if we swim here?'

'I'm not sure I want to swim anyway. It's freezing!' It was cold. It was in the low single figures still and the water temperature felt much lower as I dangled a test finger in the lake. I've been calling it a river, but I think it's a lake. The sign says so. And I don't like to argue with the Royal Parks. The Queen wouldn't be happy.

'It is cold,' I helpfully confirmed.

'We're doing this, aren't we?'

'Yep.'

'Bugger!' With that Harry glanced around to confirm that no one was watching, then he quickly ripped off his sweatshirt and removed his shoes. 'C'mon. Let's do this quick so we don't get seen.'

'That's my worry. If we start drowning I hope we are seen, really bloody quickly!' I swiftly removed all my top layers too and was pretty soon stood in just my swim shorts and what felt like a goose's plucked pimply skin.

Harry looked at my swim shorts. 'Ah. Having your swimming costume under your clothes would have been a really good idea.' He looked at his swim shorts in his hand and down at the lower half of his body. 'How am I going to do this now?'

'I dunno, but be quick. I'm f-f-freezing.'

I turned my back and Harry did a Superman quick change. We placed our clothes carefully on a nearby bench and walked gingerly over to the water.

The first toe in was weirdly like dipping your toe in boiling water. It was so cold it hurt. 'We've got to do it,' Harry said bravely stepping further into the lake. The edge of the lake had a gradual decline into the water which would have been perfect for entering the freezing water had the decline not been smeared in duck, goose and swan faeces. The decline suddenly became a wonderful death slide into the ice black water.

My mind raced with all the possibilities. How were we possibly going to get out of the lake if our exit ramp was caked in slimy grime? Maybe that sign had been there for a good reason and at the bottom of this gradual slope was a pile of frozen dead bodies that just couldn't get the underfoot purchase to get back out again. Wait, I can't feel my feet. What if I cut them on some broken glass or shard of metal? Would I know if I was bleeding? Do I have to submerge myself? If so will I be consuming this aquatic bird excrement? Isn't that how you catch bird flu? If I don't die a cold and painless death at the bottom of this lake then I will definitely die of avian flu in hospital. What a stupid way to be spending a Tuesday night!

Just when we thought things were bad, Harry fell off the edge.

The poo covered slide only went about three metres into the lake. After that it dropped dramatically down. Not deep. Only groin deep. But deep enough for Harry's testicles to drop into the freezing fluid and his singing voice to go up two octaves.

I stifled my laughter because I knew that I would have to join him in his chilly predicament.

'Hurry up,' he squeaked.

Tentatively I slid down the remainder of the crap and found the precipice. I ever so carefully stepped down to the lower level, screwing my face up and holding in my screams as the icy water enveloped my skin. I tried to stand on tip toes but the inevitable had to happen and the spuds hit the water and instantly recoiled inside me.

'I-i-i-s this enough?' Harry squealed.

'I think we've got t-t-to go under.'

'J-j-j-ust shoulders?'

'Let's just do it. Three.'

'Two.'

'One.'

We ducked under simultaneously.

We held ourselves under for what felt like and ice age but was in fact not even long enough to get wet. Immediately we started scrabbling up the dirty incline, careful not to put our hands down. Thankfully, due mainly to our frantic efforts, we managed, with much windmilling of arms, to make it to the shore. Panting for air and aching with a numbness we threw our towels round ourselves. The bottom of my feet felt strangely painful and numb at the same time. It was like I knew that standing on bare concrete should hurt but someone had forgotten to tell my feet.

My shoulders shook with cold and my teeth chattered to such an extent that my jaw muscles ached when I tried to hold my mouth shut. The vibrations travelled all the way down my body and all the way back up, but the numbness prevailed.

'That's it d-d-done,' I said when my mouth finally allowed me to speak.

Harry, who had dried himself off and was looking at the video that we had just recorded on my iPad. He looked up at me with pain in his eyes. 'It didn't work,' he groaned.

'What?' I said, all speech impediment immediately immobilised.

'The camera wasn't pointing at us when we ducked under. It was completely out of shot.'

'You are joking,' I said looking over his shoulder as he played it all again. You could hear our cries and squeals of agony but you couldn't see anything of what we had just done.

'You know what this mean?' Harry asked.

'No, we are not doing it again.'

'I think we have to, mate. And to be honest, I think we need to stay under longer.'

'Crap!'

So we did. We did the whole thing again. The whole sliding into the water over the goose muck. The whole squealing, nut dunking saga. The whole ducking under the water, only this time for five whole seconds rather than the nano-second from before and double checking that we were in shot. And the whole mad-scramble for dry land and a warm towel. We did it TWICE!

After the second time and once we had rubbed our red raw bodies with the towel which seemed to now be as rough as bark, we quickly donned our dry clothes. My body was so numb that I couldn't tell if I had put the clothes on or was just stood there in the buff. Harry attempted the Mr. Bean under towel change, whereas I adopted the quick check to see if anyone was watching, trunks down, pants on changing technique. My option were certainly quicker and had the double exhilaration of being momentarily naked in the centre of London after having been for a swim in a lake that was clearly prohibited. There wouldn't have been much to see. I'm pretty sure my gonads had become inverted in protest.

Having done the 'wild swim' we got our stuff together and went to find a restaurant for dinner. I say 'wild swim' in inverted commas because I'm not sure it really was a wild swim. We weren't fully submerged. We didn't travel anywhere in the water. It wasn't really a wild location, being the centre of the biggest city in the country. It was more of an 'urban dunk', which sounds more like a street basketball move than something that *National Geographic*'s Adventurer of the Year, Alastair Humphreys, would recommend. Was it even a microadventure?

I raised these concerns with Harry as we sat over two bowls of steaming noodles in Wagamamas.

'Yeah, course it's a microadventure. I mean, what would you be doing this evening if you hadn't been swimming in the Serpentine?'

'Probably feet up in front of the TV.'

'Exactly,' Harry beamed. 'This is a microadventure because you are doing something outside your comfort zone. It's a little bit outdoorsy. And you doing something better with your life than watching crap TV.' I love when Harry is enthusiastic about something. He makes even the least adventurous things sound exciting, rewarding and worthwhile.

'Cheers mate,' I said lifting my drink. I was thanking him for easing my mind about the validity of our microadventure and clinking glasses with him at the same time. 'What is this you ordered me anyway?' I eyed the hot brew cautiously.

'That's green tea. And that's a cococino. And this,' he said holding up his iPhone, 'is Wifi. All of these things are free in Wagamamas!' He waved his hands like this was some elaborate magic trick. To be honest I was impressed. Harry knows what a cheapskate I am. He once persuaded me to buy an item of clothing from Selfridges in London. I then spent three hours traipsing round the vast store trying to find the only item of clothing under a tenner. I'm much more of a fan of the cheap and cheerful than the ornate and expensive. Two free drinks and free internet access were right up my street.

And if nothing else at least you've learnt something new and next time you are in Wagamamas you might try the cococino. It's a warm frothy milk with a sprinkling of chocolate powder. Perfect after a freezing night dip. I hope you enjoy it.

The ecstatic high of emerging from the frigid lake was gradually being replaced by a gentle warm euphoria as we sat chatting across the table. Mutual friends again enjoying each other's company.

I'd followed some guy off the interweb. A bloke called Martin Black who seemed super super keen on microadventures. Almost fanatical. He was also making compilations about the videos that people were putting up on each of the microadventures each month. It was like a calendar of people's extra-curricular activities. It was great to see so many people were taking part in the 'Year of Microadventure' challenge.

I was flicking through one of his lists of people's different microadventures when I saw it.

Jon Doolan / Harry Francis

Jon and Harry spent a night in local woods near Bishop's Stortford, they also managed to get in the local paper!

What did we do? The local paper? Really? Wow!

Then I thought back to the previous month when I had emailed that reporter. She hadn't even emailed me back to let me know it would be published. I was a local minor celebrity and didn't even realise it.

I followed the link that Martin had kindly added to his blog and it led me to the article in full. The article told the whole story and even had a link back to Alastair's webpage as well. I felt like I was part of the circle of microadventure. Till we find our place, on the path unwinding, it's the circle, the circle of microadventure! I'm not sure Elton John would be happy with me squeezing an extra four syllables into his Lion King classic.

Anyway, I felt good to be hopefully inspiring some people to go on their own microadventures in the Hertford, Ware and Bishops Stortford area. And also giving them the links to find out everything they need to know in the same way I had. It's a warm fuzzy feeling when something like this happens.

March

Ok, so maybe February's microadventure was a bit of a cheat. I felt great after doing it. I mean, I was ill for a week afterwards, but I felt invincible. I felt that nothing could stop me (apart from tiny bacteria) in my quest to become a real microadventurer. I was a militant disciple to Al's call to arms. Using the local media, social media and word of mouth I was spreading the joy of wild camping and microadventures in general.

Harry was out of the country touring round Europe showing off his business at various trading shows like a big ugly corporate prostitute. He told me he had a cracking time and I was a wee bit jealous of his multi-national escapades but I had an ace up my sleeve.

Alastair Humphreys, the guy who'd written the Microdventures book, was holding a 'Night of Adventure' in a lecture theatre at UCL. It was to raise money for the charity that he supports, Hope and Homes for Children.

I buzzed my younger brother, Rob, a text to see if he could make it, which he could so we met just outside the tube at Russell Square before heading over to the venue. Rob knew one of the charity workers from a previous job so got chatting to her while I milled around the stalls checking out all the speakers' books and reading up on their travels.

The lecture was superb because it had a mad format where each presentation was just twenty slides which skip along after twenty seconds whether the speaker is ready or not. This caught a few of the adventurers out but made for ten fast and enjoyably motivating speeches. Some of the adventures were mental, like a girl who circumnavigated Wales with a donkey or another who showed twenty photos of him skinny dipping (I ended up buying his book!)

At the interval I scooted down to the front and waited patiently while Alastair was chatting away amicably with a fellow adventure enthusiast. I was like a teenage girl in front of a pop star, all wobbly knees and stuttering. Here he was the object of my current obsession, just a normal friendly guy who was smiling and chatting.

Eventually I caught his eye and he beckoned me over. 'Hi,' I stammered nervously.

'Hi,' he responded smiling politely.

What was I going to say? How do you talk to someone who has inspired you to do things you have never done before. I say I was a little bewildered would be like saying Coldplay are a little bit depressing, i.e. a massive understatement.

'Yes?' Alastair encouraged, still smiling politely. I realised that I'd been thinking about how lovely a smile he had. I'd forgotten to actually say anything.

'Oh... um, please can I take a selfie with you. I have a friend who I've been doing microadventures with and he'd be really jealous if I showed him a picture with me and you in it.' The sentence fell out of my mouth in a rapid blurb of noise. I'm surprised that I managed to annunciate any of the consonants in between the vowels. I was becoming more tongue-tied than a chameleon boy scout who'd been using his tongue for rope practice.

'Sure,' he said and put his arm round me for the photo. I was all fingers and thumbs like Thing from the Addams Family and couldn't work my phone for the selfie. Finally I took a blurry shot of the two of us standing there. I thanked Alastair profusely and returned to my seat, giddy at our first encounter.

With only a few words he'd been a kind, welcoming and charming man. The vibes coming off of him confirm that he is definitely a good person with his heart in the right place and definitely a chap to spend a year emulating.

Rob looked at my beaming face quizzically as I returned to my seat and we enjoyed the second half of adventurous speakers. I text Harry the photo immediately and he responded equally quickly with a simple answer.

Well jeal!

Admittedly, Harry and I had only been on one wild camp in two months. Admittedly we hadn't really attempted a mid-week '5-to-9' microadventure, the cornerstone of Al's philosophy. I felt great for having done something but also like we had cheated the system. We hadn't even camped at all last time.

Basically what Al (by the way, he's called Al now. We're on first name terms after we met. We're pretty much best buds) wants with the '5-to-9' adventure is for us to use our time on this earth more effectively. What he asks of us is 'What do you do in the hours between 5pm and 9am each day?' Most of us probably have a sensible answer, like go home, watch a soap, go to bed, get up, have a shower and go to work. Pretty reasonable, right? What are you doing tonight? Something along those lines I bet.

What Al suggests is that we could do so much more with our mid-week nights. We are at work between the hours of 9am and 5pm. Eight hours of hard graft, manual labour, whatever. The other sixteen hours, the hours between 5pm and 9am, are ours to do with what we like. So why not jump on a train and head out to the countryside and go and camp on a hill? Why not jump on a bike and cycle into the wilderness? Why not jump in your car and find yourself on a clifftop by morning?

I'll tell you why not, Al. First off, I am a teacher. I don't know a single teacher worth their salt who doesn't work from 8am to 6pm when the caretaker is locking up the building and shoving you out the door. Even if they do leave work at 3.30pm they'd have to take a lot of marking, lesson planning etc. home with them. The time frame is impossible to work with.

Secondly, even if you do get away at 5pm and you're up to date with all your paperwork (HA!) then you haven't factored in the amount of time it takes to get changed into outdoor stuff. The time it takes to get to where you are meant to be meeting your camping companion is also non-existent. When you live on one end of London and your bivvying buddy is on the far end of London you don't have a hope in hell of meeting up until after dark.

Cut to me pulling my Volvo into a spare space at Harry's new apartment in Leighton Buzzard. He had moved out of his ex-girlfriend's flat which had alleviated a lot of the awkwardness. The sun was just sinking below the horizon leaving the Buzz in gloomy twilight.

Harry greeted me with a big bag on his back a wide grin on his face and a brand new shiny wok in his grubby grip. 'Do you like my wok, Jon?'

'Didn't expect to be answering that question tonight,' I laughed.

'Shiny isn't it,' he caressed the curves of the pan lovingly. He had a worryingly adoring look in his eye.

'Ok. I give in. What is the wok for?'

'I'm going to cook you dinner in the woods!'

I had a mixed feeling to this revelation. On the one hand I was really excited about the opportunity to cook food outdoors. Maybe we'd have a fire. Would we be like scouts catching squirrels and roasting them over a spit? Would we be baking our own bread on a stick or digging baked potatoes from the ashes? Who would be playing the guitar while we sing Kumbaya?

On the other hand, was this wise? It was already late. I had no idea where we were heading. Did we have time to make a fire, cook our food and put it out? Were we likely to start a forest fire? Also, Harry, for a profession is a food entrepreneur. This basically means that he prats around with food inventions. Was he just about to unleash one of his lunatic contraptions on me? Was I to be his guinea pig?

'So I've got a little camp stove...'

'Ok that makes a lot of sense.' Phew. No forest fires.

'... and a pack of prawns. I'm making you a stir fry.'

'Not *raw* prawns.'

'Yes, raw prawns.'

Oh dear.

Harry's flat backed onto the canal. He'd go running down the canal for an after work de-stress. He said that in the daylight it was lovely. I'd have to take his word for this. As we crunched along the gravel tow path all I could make out of the canal was a black flat surface. Every now and again the stillness was broken by a wandering duck as it skated across the surface leaving behind a 'V'-shaped wake in its... wake.

The odd narrow boat was dotted along the canal. Some of them glowed from the inside. Little shards of warm light escaped from the edges of curtains or shutters. They looked like cosy little floating cottages on this cool evening.

The Globe Inn was even more enticing. A couple of lads stood outside having a smoke in the lamplight from the pub and the gentle welcoming murmur of voices could be heard from the open door. Looking through the windows we could see people laughing and joking, sharing a pint and story. It looked very inviting to stop for a bit, but we knew we already had our dinner in Harry's rucksack.

Basically, everywhere was looking more inviting than sleeping outside.

We tore ourselves away from the aroma of a warm cooked dinner and Harry tried to persuade me that he was going to make a meal that was going to surpass the local fare in the pub. It was touch and go for a minute though. I almost had one foot in the door before I turned back.

We trudged on for what seemed an age. We left the canal and followed a pitch black country road and tried not to get run over by racing cars with blindingly bright headlights. On and on we walked.

'Where are we actually going, mate?'

'Just a bit further.'

We eventually arrived at a gate. We followed the dirt track for a little while and then headed up a steep wooded hill. We seemed a very long way from the pub, and even further from my car. Was this walk ever going to end?

And then it did. 'This will do,' said Harry flinging down his pack. The wok clanged against a root. We'd stopped at the summit of a hill. Downhill from us, where we had walked from, was a dense wood carpeted with brown detritus. In the other direction an empty dark field stretched out for the entirety of the downward slope. Just beyond that the lights of a train sped through the night.

The ground was covered in last season's ferns that had browned and softened to create a wonderful soft cushion. It made for interesting walking because it was difficult to see the divots and roots as everything was carpeted in the same colour. I felt like the family in 'Going on a Bear Hunt' who 'Stumble, Trip. Stumble, Trip' all the way through the deep dark woods. It was lovely to lay our roll mats out on a soft crunchy mattress of broken bracken once we had found a relatively flat area.

I kicked aside some of the dried ferns and the new shoots that were just appearing to make a muddy patch. There is an ethos in wild camping to leave the site as you found it but I think that a few dead fern plants was a small price to pay to have a safe fire. And besides, the ferns would grow back pretty quickly.

I was remembering back to my days as a scout when we went on camp, or even one of the many programmes that Ray Mears has made about outdoor survival. I felt like a proper pro, right back in nature, honing my natural skills. It was the call of the wild.

Then Harry got out his gas stove. The whole one-with-nature mood was lost when the unnatural blue flames licked into life with a hiss. Nevermind.

Harry dropped the wok on top of the stove and flung the raw grey prawns on top. They sizzled and spat and the grey shellfish gradually turned pink. He tossed some veg and noodles on top and then added a packet sauce. He let it bubble away for a few minutes before handing me a fork. We ate from the pan, like proper cavemen, slurping the greasy noodles and crunching on the pak choi.

As meals go it wasn't the best. There was insufficient sauce to cover all the veg and noodles. The host had forgotten to supply any beverages so we were stuck with water. But I liked the company and the view was nice, so I am going to give Harry a 6.

Harry chucked everything in a plastic bag. He'd brought everything apart from the kitchen sink so we couldn't wash up.

After the slap up dinner we snuggled up into our bivvys and lay and looked up at the sky. Again the moon was out and bright. As I moved my head it played hide and seek between the branches. Harry bemoaned the fact that his sleeping bag was, in his words, a Hawaiian season sleeping bag and offered him next to no warmth at all, while my four season made me snug as a bug in a rug. Do you remember the feeling when you were a kid (or a student) and you came downstairs wrapped in your duvet and sat watching TV? That's approximately how snug I felt. No imagine you don't have a sofa but have to sit on the floor. That's probably a bit closer.

Harry pulled his hat down over his face and pulled his scarf tighter around his neck and was snoring in next to no time at all.

And I just lay there.

For ages.

Then the stomach cramps started. Like hot daggers to the gut. Like an invisible hand had reached into my abdomen and was gripping my intestines and pulling them apart. My stomach gurgled ominously. I needed to fart so bad but I daren't. My butt hole ached from clenching it tight shut. I rolled on my side and clenched my arms around my core in a desperate attempt to stop my insides from exploding out. Sudden sharp jabs of pain injected in my middle.

I contemplated getting up, staggering off into the dark and emptying my bowels on some poor tree but I had no means of wiping my behind. I didn't want to wake Harry with my inevitable butt trumpet. I didn't know if I could go far enough away to ensure the stench didn't waft over us for the rest of the night. I was in a dilemma.

I scrunched up into the foetal position and stifled a moan so as not to wake my unconscious pal. Pal? More like poisoner! I tried not to move too much as the ferns underneath me crunched and crumbled. The agony was intense. I screwed my eyes shut and tried to ignore the pain. It was impossible.

This went on for about four hours.

Eventually I must have dropped off because I woke to a pale sun creeping above the horizon. That can't be right I thought. I'd set my alarm for 5.30am so that I would have enough time to walk back to the car and drive to work. I looked at my watch. 6.27.

6.27!! Aaaaah!

'Quick! Get up! We're late!' I screamed at Harry.

He rolled over and looked at me with sleepy, unintelligible eyes.

'C'mon. We've got to go now.'

I leapt out of my sleeping bag and started ramming it unceremoniously into its stuff sack. Harry to his credit started responding very swiftly and had his own bivvy and sleeping packed in moments. We rapidly deflated our roll mats and were trudging down the wooded slope in less than five minutes.

That's one of the best things about wild camping. There's no cursed tent to take down and pack away. You simply chuck the whole sleeping bag / bivvy combo into a stuff sack, roll up your mat and away you go. You're even fully dressed in all your clothes so you don't have to bother with that unnecessary morning task.

I remember when I was a teenager once. I had decided that putting school uniform on in the morning was an extra hassle that I didn't need and could mean I had an extra-long lie in. One evening I decided to have my shower and go to bed fully dressed in shirt and trousers ready for the morning. I think I would have got away with it had my form tutor not suspected that I wasn't being looked after at home properly. That was an awkward conversation with my mum.

Now, as a legitimate adult, I could go out and sleep in my clothes and no teachers would be able to grass me up. Get in!

So, anyway, we were trudging down the hill, weren't we? This is when the really bad thing happened. The thing that is the worst thing to ever happen to me on a microadventure, ever!

I sharted.

For those who aren't up with the latest slanguage in the urban dictionary 'sharted' is a mixture between the words 'farted' and… well… you can probably guess.

In my mad panic to get going that morning I had completely forgotten the whole reason why I was late getting up in the first place, i.e. the lack of sleep from having a dicky tummy. As I was tramping down the hill I was also trumping as well, and one of those trumps had followed through. I could feel the wetness in my pants. It was really unpleasant to say the least. Quite literally, it felt crap.

'I think I've just pooed myself!' I told Harry alarmed.

'What? Just then?'

'Yep.' I explained how I had been up all night with stomach cramps and how I couldn't have gone to the toilet because we didn't have any toilet paper and I didn't want to wake him by doing the number two nearby. 'It was those bloody prawns you fed me last night. I knew raw prawns were a big mistake.'

'Ah, mate. You should have asked. I had toilet roll.'

'What?'

'And in the night when I needed a wee I just stood on my roll mat and weed off into the dark.'

'With me just lying there?'

'Yep.'

'Mate, that's gross.'

'Says the man who just pooed his pants.'

'Fair point.'

I waddled the rest of the way down the hill with Harry chuckling behind me. I looked at my watch again. I was going to be so late for work.

We sped along the track, through the gate, down the country lanes and made it to the canal. How far had we walked the night before? It seemed like a ridiculously long time and it felt even longer on the way back with a time constraint and brown mess leaking in my undergarments.

I'm sure I would have enjoyed the serene canal with the gentle mist tickling the surface. Or the calm swans gliding, breaking the calm waters into a rippling magic mirror. Or the elegant tweeting of the dawn chorus as if the birds were singing us on down the gravel track. Or the horse nuzzling in the field nearby his breath distilling in a cloud of steam in the air. Or even the erratic speed of the early commuter trains racing and rattling past. If only I didn't have poo in my pants and wasn't sweating like a wrestler in five layers of fleeces.

Harry jogging along beside me. He was far too lively and awake breaking the silence with his foghorn voice as he greeted the morning sunshine.

I was going to be so late for work.

Together we sprinted across the car park to my Volvo and I threw my camping gear in the boot. I tugged off three or four sweaty layers and threw them in the boot too. (Just realised that if you put the word 'brick' in the middle of that last sentence it takes on whole new meaning!)

Harry and I had a brief farewell and I gunned the engine and roared through the sleepy streets of Leighton Buzzard, carefully sticking to all speed limits and road signage, of course officer.

Then I sat in traffic, in my soiled underwear, for two hours!

Meanwhile Harry went back to bed, the lazy sod.

I arrived at work with ten minutes to spare before I had to register my form class. I peeled off my cack stained underwear in the staff showers and rinsed the crusty poo balls from my bum in a lovely warm shower. I was clean at last.

As I stepped out of the shower room and into my office my work colleagues looked at me as one.

'Jon,' said my boss Shane, 'When you walked passed the office earlier it stank like you'd rolled in shit.'

Oh dear.

April

I'd had to fess up to everything at work. It had been awkward and I'd deservedly won the 'Clown Award', a ridiculously elaborate engraved shield, for the term. But time passed and people forgot about it.

No, they didn't! They reminded me every day! It emphatically enforced their opinion that I was an absolute lunatic for sleeping out under the stars on a school night. At least they'd stopped insisting that I was going to be buggered by a badger. I suppose the very real threat of excreting in your own underwear outweighs the highly improbable situation of sodomy with a woodland critter.

So April came round and Harry and I decided that we'd do something a little bit different for this month. I'd invested in the steadfastly most used piece of gear any self-respecting YouTuber needs, the ubiquitous selfie stick. As budding film makers we had a think about how we could present the videos of our microadventures in a more interesting way and struck on the idea of a music video. I don't know why, I think we were just a bit bored of putting videos of us stumbling around in darkness.

I called Harry to see if he had any ideas of a song.

'Maybe, Uptown Funk?' he suggested. 'It's current.'

'That's good but we don't know all the words.'

'Good point.'

'What about Queen or the Beatles?' I said.

'Doesn't really relate to us.'

'Fair enough. So we need a song that we both know all the words to and is a song that relates to us.'

'I'll have a think.'

'By the way, my brother Rob really wants to come on our next microadventure.' I said. Rob, the fourth brother of five, is probably the most keen outdoorsman. He loves sailing and camping and travelling. He'd been inspired by Al's 'Night of Adventure' lecture back in March and wanted to get out there and give this microadventure thing a go. Rob works in London for a logistics company or something or other. Or was it for a charity? I don't remember. I told you our family wasn't that close.

Rob was the sort of guy who takes his brother to musicals, enjoys baking and has done a few tours on the tall ships. He's practically in the navy, if you know what I mean.

'Yeah, that's great.'

'Oh, and he wants to bring his mate.'

'Sure, whatever. The more the merrier. So where should we go?'

'I dunno. We could go wherever, you know. I mean, I've always wanted to sleep on a beach. Maybe somewhere on the east coast. If it was somewhere like Southend-on-sea, then we could get a train there from Stratford. The 5.43 train would get us into Southend at 6.38.'

'You've made the decision already, haven't you?'

'We could eat fish and chips on the beach,' I coerced him.

'Sold!'

Two weeks later found me desperately driving up the M11 towards home. Completely the wrong direction. I was meant to be driving towards central London, towards Westfield shopping centre where I had planned to leave my car for the night before hopping on the train at Stratford to head to the salty air of the seaside town of Southend.

My phone buzzed in the hands free cradle on my windscreen. I hit the reply button and the loud speaker. 'I'm driving,' I screamed at the phone.

'Ok,' said Rob sounding a little scared, 'I was just wondering what the plan is.'

Bollocks. I'd forgotten that I was going to meet Rob and his mate at Stratford. 'Ah, crap. Sorry Rob. I've had to drive home first. I don't think I am going to make the train at Stratford.'

'We are still doing a microadventure?'

'Yeah, defo. Just got to go home first. I've forgotten something.'

Forgotten something is an understatement. I was suffering from one of the biggest Third World crises. My whole middle class life was about to come crashing down around my ears. My wife would never have forgiven me if I hadn't raced home and rectified this massive dilemma. My life would not have been worth living.

I'd forgotten to leave the money out for the cleaner!

I know. It's a disaster, isn't it?

I mean, I could quite conceivably have rung the cleaner and told her that I'd pay her next time, or that she didn't have to bother coming in tomorrow but I didn't have the cleaner's number. Sally did.

I could've rung my neighbour, who has a spare key, and asked them to drop some cash round. They would have been more than happy I'm sure. But then Sally would have found out.

No. I had to sort this out myself.

Why the effort to drive thirty miles in the wrong direction you may ask. Why miss a rendezvous with my brother and his pal that would have seen me sat on a train, cracking open a can of beer with my feet on the opposite chair enjoying the relaxing feeling of being whisked off to my next adventure without care in the world? Why indeed.

Because I had told Sally that my microadventures would have no impact on her whatsoever. Because she was starting to get tired of my enthusiasm for taking part in activities that didn't involve her or our daughter. Because I was about a thousand times less enthusiastic about walking to the shops or sitting in coffee shops with her, which it seemed was all we were doing in our free time.

Mainly because I didn't want to be told off.

'Sam and I will still get the train, shall we?' Rob's detached voice floated around the inside of my car.

'Yeah, do that. I'll try and meet you on the train at Basildon or somewhere.'

'See you then.' Rob definitely sounded like someone who felt like he was about to be stood up.

'Bollocks,' I muttered to my steering wheel once I had terminated the call.

Arriving in, I checked the train times. If I had left three minutes earlier I could have still made it back to Stratford in time but it would have been far too close. I threw the cash on the breakfast counter and flew out the door. What a waste of a drive.

I immediately found Harry's contact and the phone was ringing tinnily in its cradle as I backed out of my drive.

'Helloozzles,' said the unerringly happy chappy.

'Mate, I'm not going to make the train,' I came clean.

'No worries, neither am I.' He seemed rather nonchalant about it.

'I thought you were meeting us in Stratford.'

'Nope. Can't make it. I'm going to drive all the way to Southend.' Typical Harry.

'Well neither can I. I've had a right palaver here. I'm going to drive to Basildon which is about halfway and meet Rob and his mate, Sam, there.'

'Oh, ok. Why don't I meet you at Basildon?'

'Do you think this conversation is getting a bit boring?'

'Yes. Definitely.'

'Do you think we should just stop it now?'

'Probably, I don't think anyone would be bothered to read it if you wrote it in a book.'

'No, they would have probably stopped this bit and skipped onto the next paragraph.'

'Well if they haven't I'm sure they will now have by now.' So I ended the call.

We met in Basildon. I parked my car in a long stay car park near the station, taking special note of the fact that the car park wasn't locked overnight, just in case. The ticket ran out at six the next morning. Didn't seem a problem.

After various unnecessarily confusing triangulating calls with Harry, I eventually found him on the other side of the train station looking like a disco tramp in his oversized luminous yellow ski jacket and green bobble hat.

Mere minutes later Rob arrived.

With a girl.

Sam was a girl. Ok. Hadn't anticipated that. 'This is Sam,' said Rob introducing us.

I hate meeting girls that I don't know. That awkward moment just after you have been introduced. Do you shake hands? Do you embrace? Do you go for a kiss on the cheek? And once you've made the decision, how do you communicate with the person opposite you? What if she proffers and hand and I go in for a peck? And the man should lead on this as well, which is massively sexist in my opinion. Whatever you do will decide how close you are for the rest of your encounter. And we were planning to sleep on a beach together. This was even more awkward than necessary.

On a separate note, have you noticed how awkward the word awkward looks when written down? No? Maybe it's just me.

So I proffered a hand, which she shook.

And Harry laid a smacker on her cheek. So he won.

She seemed nice enough. A bit quiet but maybe she was taken aback by Harry and my uncontrollable enthusiasm to hit the road and get some serious miles under our wheels. We still had a way to go before we reached Southend.

We all bundled into Harry's car, Harry and I sharing a wry smile, and headed to the coast.

'So did you come up with a song?' I asked Harry.

'I have got the perfect song,' he replied as he fiddled with his iPod.

From the first guitar note I knew the song. It had been the rock song that had defined our first year of university. The stupid lyrics. The ridiculous tale told in song. The comically excessive vocals of Jack Black. The completely unexpected a cappella yodel half way through. The extreme guitar solo. Pure idiotic fresher fodder.

On campus most days you could hear Tenacious D blaring out of either my or Harry's rooms. The immature pair pretending to be funny, pretending to be cool, failing on all accounts. It could have been Jack and Kyle or it could have been me and Harry. At least they could rock on their guitars while we just sat in our rooms harmonising the yodel.

Now it all paid off as we sat in the car blasting out the song at the top of our voices while Rob and his female compatriot sat in the back seats with a fixed perplexed look on their faces. When the song came to the end I tried to reassure Sam that this isn't typically what we did on a microadventure, though Rob did affirm that we did normally do this sort of random rubbish.

The road trip from Basildon, locally known as Bas Vegas, to Southend passed in a blur of rock, screaming the words at the top of our lungs and marvelling at the rapidity of the sunset. Once again, it seemed, we'd be completing our microadventure in darkness.

As we drove through the dreary dark streets of the coastal town we looked up at the quiet houses and shops. The metal shutters were drawn on almost all of the shop fronts. I wasn't sure whether this was because of the late hour or because so many small businesses had folded since the recession. The only building that seemed to have its lights on was the UKIP centre on the waterfront which was the busiest place in town. It's no wonder in the elections that came that following May that UKIP won their only seat in Southend when they are the only shop that is open.

That wasn't entirely true. The UKIP centre was lit up by a bright purple boarding above the door but it wasn't the only place that was still awake. Harry pulled his hatchback over on the esplanade and we strolled along the silent street until we found some life in this lifeless town. It was so eerie being in a resort town which is designed for the buzz and excitement of hundreds of holidaying Essexites (a word which is apparently real according to the spell check on my laptop!). But there was virtually no one here. It was completely drained. Like the exuberance and fun had been sucked out of it. It was like a juicy grape turned into a crusty raisin. Like a retired showgirl with her make up wiped off. Like a shiny coin that was scuffed, pitted and rusted on the pavement.

So we found it a bit shocking when we walked round a corner and stood in the dazzling crossfire or two rival arcades that were either side of a thoroughfare. The bright illuminations glared at each other from across the way. The cuddly toys hanging above the machines smiled benignly. The 'grab-a-teddy' cranes hung idly in their clear Perspex cases. I imagined one arcade run by Italian mafia staring across the street polishing their tommy guns while the Chinese triad sat opposite sharpening their katanas. We had a quick go on the cranes in the arcade on the left but, with fears of waking up in the middle of the night with a horse's head by our bivvy bags, we headed across the road and spent a couple of quid on the machines there. It would be a complete lie if I said that we weren't enticed to separate ourselves from more of our cash but we needed to go and find a chippy that was still open or all four of us would go hungry that night.

We wandered the streets looking for a fish shop but we had no luck. We asked a local, the only guy who wasn't a skinhead walking a bulldog or Rottweiler, for directions to an eatery but, just like every other shopfront on the high street, the shutters were down and it was well and truly closed. I suppose seaside chip shops don't really have a roaring trade on a Wednesday evening in April.

We trekked across town until we found the only fish shop that was still open. The lovely Cantonese lady behind the counter served us quickly and even danced for us in our video, which was sweet. She was a bit confused about why four young people in woolly hats had invaded her quiet takeaway and were dancing about the tiled floor to a tinny rock song that was playing off of one of their phones.

'For *Cod*'s sake!' exclaimed Harry through a mouthful of steaming potato slices as we strolled back to the arcades. 'These are the best chips I've ever tasted.'

Let the game commence, I thought. The Pun Game. The rules are simple. Keep making puns. When someone can't or their pun is just unbearable they lose.

'That was the best *plaice* in town to get chips.' I retaliated sucking grease from my fingers.

'You *batter* believe it!'

'The *sole* reason I came to Southend was for these chips.'

'It is the best chippy in this *roe* of shops.'

'That young lady behind the counter, I bet she's just like her dad. She's a *chip* off the old block.'

'If I beat you in this game don't have a *chip* on your shoulder.'

'I wish I'd got a milks-*hake* with my meal.'

'That pun was *pollocks*.'

'I hope Rob remembered his sleeping bag. *Eel* have a bad sleep tonight if he didn't'

'I've *haddock* up to here with these puns.'

'I wish you would stop *carp*-ing on.'

'*Salmon* these puns are just awful.'

We stood under a lamppost slowly filling our faces with hot chips looking into the middle distance desperately trying to fit the name of a fish into a sentence. We often have these strange silences, Harry and I. Just stood there. Thinking of puns. Is that normal?

'Come on John,' said Harry before adding, 'Dory,' under his breath.

He'd won. Bollocks. As Harry would tell you, I am not competitive at all. In fact I am the least competitive person I know, so I win! (I wish I could take credit for this joke. I can't. It's from Family Guy.)

Winning means nothing to me, unless it's me doing it in which case winning is everything. I wasn't gutted that I'd lost to Harry. I was devastated.

I screwed the paper the chips had come in into a tight ball and threw it in a bin from a distance of about twelve foot. I gave a tiny fist pump that Harry couldn't see and strolled on nonchalantly.

Rob and Sam had been with us for the whole time but had wisely kept a safe distance as we had spent most of the evening dancing down the street singing to Tenacious D. In light of our surroundings and the local residents, the youths on the benches on the high street and the man in a tight white t-shirt on a cold spring night who looked like he lifted buses for a living, they were probably being quite wise. I'm sure the crazy-haired old cat lady wheeling her shopping trolley and muttering to herself seemed saner than we did as we jumped around pole-dancing lampposts and hopping over bollards.

We made it back to the two rival arcades and while Rob and Sam had another stab at the predictably fruitless but addictive crane machines, Harry and I made ourselves busy shooting some extra footage in the arcade, getting told off by a bouncer who was literally as wide as a phone box and jumping around on Noddy's car that sat forlornly on the pavement outside. Our thirst for gambling and pratting around sated we headed back to the car.

Southend had not really lived up to our expectations. It was a drab, soulless place full of scary people who you could definitely imagine would sign up to a White Supremacy campaign or join the Nazi party. The only redeeming feature had been the lovely Cantonese lady but she didn't really seem representative of the area. Maybe when seeing a coastal town late at night on a weekday, out of season, I should expect it not be shown in its best light. But Southend had really disappointed us and we saw no reason we should stay and camp there. We all climbed back inside the Harrymobile and drove along the coast out of town.

All along the beach they were doing work. Later I found out, from my boss' mum who lives just up the coast, that they were digging sand up that was out to sea and dumping it on the beach to make the beach bigger for the summer. Seemed like a lot of effort and meant that most of the beach was fenced off, which buggered up our plans to sleep on it.

We drove east until the steel construction fences stopped and pulled up down a small road into a deserted, dark car park. We felt a little clandestine as the signs everywhere said 'Road Closed' and 'Car Park Closed' but we weren't doing anyone any harm and we'd be gone before the sun came up. We donned head torches and pulled together our gear out of Harry's boot and headed across a field toward the beach. The wind was blowing a cool salty breeze from the sea which was refreshing on the face but worrying when we thought that we might need shelter. The throb of a red light from a nearby mast illuminated the cloudy sky.

There's a lot of people out there who bemoan the light pollution sent out by the vast swathes of populated Britain. There's still places, so called 'Dark Sky Spots', that you can find throughout the UK if you go searching for them. I know that recently Al spent a night in Exmoor to try and catch a glimpse of the Perseid meteor shower. As Al found, being in a 'Dark Sky Spot' is no guarantee of a beautiful starlit sky if it's destined to be a cloudy night. Bit of a waste of time going all the way to Devon to sit in a bank of fog if you ask me.

For my part I completely agree. Being amazed by the majesty of the heavens is incomparable. Seeing the dying light of a million suns a million miles away does nothing but inspire and awe me. It also makes me a little bit sad as I realise just how insignificant I am in the vast grand scheme of things. It also makes me realise just how insignificant my worries are and so acts as a cathartic stress relief. Whoever wrote the nursery rhyme 'Twinkle, twinkle, little star,' was sat there staring at the same sky you and I both live under. Whoever he was, he was in equal parts genius and moron. The simplicity of the wonder and amazement of gazing at the starry night sky is encapsulated in the basic lyrics. But I could do without listening to it on EVERY car journey while my daughter is sat in the back of the car. I literally sing it in my sleep.

So starry skies are wonderful and glorious but if it is going to be overcast there is nothing better than the unnatural glow of an industrial district. Sounds counter intuitive? It's not. The warm orange glow that emanates across the land is comforting. The fluorescent brightness of the sky as it reflects street lights enables you to see without the necessity of a head torch which is liberating in itself. The radiance of local homes, businesses and factories make it slightly less ominous camping out in the middle of nowhere.

The Thames estuary was perfect.

The only concern is that it looks a little like the sky is on fire. I imagine that the Great Fire of London started with Samuel Pepys looking out his window at a cloudy night sky and worrying about his electricity bill.

We threw out our inflatable roll mats on a grassy hill above the beach. We'd contemplated sleeping on the sand but realised that the high tide mark was above the sea wall. We didn't fancy waking up in the middle of the night drifting out sea. Would have made the commute back to work in the morning a struggle.

'I'm going to be late to work.'

'Why's that?'

'I've accidentally floated to Denmark.'

Snuggling down into our sleeping bags we wished each other a good night's sleep and lay back silently staring up at the ruddy sky. That's ruddy as in red, not ruddy as in the sky was being particular annoying.

'Jon,' Harry suddenly rolled over and shook me out of my slumber.

'What?'

'I think I'm sleeping on a bees' nest!'

'What?' I said a little more awake.

'Can't you hear that buzzing?'

I lay motionless. 'What buzzing?' What was he talking about?

'It must be under my roll mat,' Harry said scuttling to one side.

I pressed my ear to his mat. There was complete silence. Maybe these wild camps had finally sent him insane. Maybe he was picking up a signal from the nearby radio mast. Maybe Harry is just odd.

'I can still hear the buzzing!'

It's probably that Harry is just odd.

'Look, you can sleep on my mat,' I offered and we switched places.

'I can still hear it. You must be able to hear it!'

'Go to sleep, Harry.'

We both lay back down and Harry eventually stopped fidgeting and went to sleep.

The alarm on my watch beeped repeatedly at 4.30am.
4 bloody 30!
In the morning!
'Why so early?' you may ask. Maybe you didn't. Well, I'm telling you anyway. I hadn't anticipated how far Basildon was from Southend. It's an hour drive. We needed to get packed up, walk back to the car and drive all the way to Basildon before 6am. That's when my car park ticket ran out. It would be just my luck some anal ticket inspector would be sat, ticket book in hand, pencil poised, glaring at my Volvo. Bastard! I bet he's got beady little eyes with thick glasses and a greasy comb-over. Dirty grotty ticket man!

'Surely there won't be a car park attendant working at 6am,' you may say. Maybe you didn't. Maybe I'm having a conversation with myself. Isn't that the first sign of madness? Maybe this camping malarkey is sending me bonkers as well as Harry.

Maybe you're right (or I'm right, or we're right... this is getting complicated). Maybe there won't be a sweaty bloke gripping a ticket hovering over my windscreen impatiently glowering at the second hand as it slowly tick by on his wristwatch. Maybe. But maybe I couldn't risk it.

I'd promised my wife, Sally, that the microadventures would have absolutely zero impact on her life. She'd been complaining that I'd been way too focused on my adventures. Apparently I'd been shoving it in her face. I'd been massively enthusiastic about my time doing the things I wanted to do. Time that was apart from her and our daughter, Rosie. I'd been making it seem like I enjoyed being away from them more than I enjoyed being with them. On top of this I had been hugely exhausted from work so by the time the weekend came round I was falling asleep on the sofa or snuggling up on the floor with Rosie. I'd had no energy and no enthusiasm.

I guess Sally was jealous of my time away. I kept telling her that she could have time off from me and Rosie too but she kept telling me that all she wanted to do was spend time with us both. This only served to make me feel even guiltier for enjoying my time apart.

I was a melting pot of joy and guilt. I was also probably a little bit in fear of the wrath of Sally should I go back on my word about the microadventures impacting on her life. Imagine how much hell would have broken loose if she had opened a brown envelope in the post that let her know that I'd received a £50 parking fine. Do not pass go. Do not collect £200. I'll give you a clue how much hell. All of it!

So I would rather make myself, my best mate, my brother and a random girl get up at 4.30 in the morning than be on the wrong side of Sally's anger. Is that ridiculous? I feel like I'm a bit of wuss. At least I think I've got my priorities right.

We stumbled through the semi-dark down to the beach. Harry and I had contemplated going for an early morning swim but a look out over the dark waves as they came crashing up the sand made my goosebumps shiver. The wind whipping cold salty water into the air at this ungodly hour did not inspire me to strip down to my boxers and go diving into the saline froth. No, I was quite happy to be stood in four jumpers, a woolly hat and a warm scarf wrapped tightly around my freezing chin, thank you very much. Al champions an early morning swim but I must admit, I find him more and more bonkers the more I indulge in these microadventures of his. He's more crackers than a box of broken Jacobs biscuits stuck up a builder's bum!

Harry and I danced a little dance on the beach to the now repetitive Tenacious D song. The lyrics were engrained on our brains like mould in a blue cheese. I was surprised that we hadn't started miming it in our sleep. All four of us tramped up the footpath back to the car park laboriously. We wedged our gear back in the boot and clambered into the hatchback.

The two in the back instantaneously fell asleep. They looked like a pair of those nodding dog things you used to see on the back shelves of Ford Fiestas back in the day as their heads bobbed back and forth in rhythm to the turns of the road. I desperately fought off the urge to close my eyes as I tried to keep our driver, Harry, awake and save us all from flaming oblivion. We pootled down the country roads until we linked up again with the A12 and home.

Or not. Because I wasn't heading home. Once I'd been dropped off by Harry at my car in Basildon I had to get all the way back to work. I offered to drop Rob and Sam at a tube station near my school which they gladly accepted as it meant that they could continue their nap in the back of the car while I listened intently to the morning show on Radio 4 to try and keep my brain engaged and prevent the slip into the land of nod. I dutifully dropped Rob and Sam at the underground station and carried on to work. I stumbled into the office, bleary eyed and dishevelled, made my way gratefully to the shower room and stood underneath the jet of lukewarm water until I felt almost human again.

It took some time.

May

Harry put the video together for the Tenacious D / Southend-on-Sea microadventure from April. It looked great, though once again virtually all of the shots were in the dark. As we were getting closer to the middle of the year and the summer solstice I hoped that our videos would be a bit more viewer friendly with a few more shots in daylight.

May's microadventure was the most spontaneous of all. We'd fixed a date well in advance but had left all the details until the very last moment. That's one of the great things about these microadventures. They take almost zero organisation. I now had a bag that was ready to go each month. Like an espionage 'Go-bag' but instead of cash and a passport, my bag had a few wild camping essentials. Just a small backpack filled with a sleeping bag with a liner already inside and a bivvy already on the outside. This saved so much time when setting up camp and saved loads of space in my backpack because it all packs down really small in one of those stuff bags. The only other things in there are a torch, one of my daughter's toothbrushes with a travel size toothpaste, a spare fleece, a woolly hat and, my one luxury that I allow myself, a tiny travel pillow. Other things have been thrown in and out depending on the adventure. If I am the one doing the filming I will bring a gorilla pod for my iPhone, my GoPro and a selfie stick. I also had a lighter and tin foil in there in case we made a fire. We hadn't done so far but I really wanted to do it. Finally, attached to the outside of the bag is a blow up roll mat and, having learnt our lessons from the first microadventure, a bottle of water.

That was literally it. I didn't need a change of clothes because I slept in my clothes. This also makes getting up in the morning so much easier.

Harry sent me a text on the morning of the microadventure. Neither of us had forgotten about the microadventure. Both of us were still really excited about it. But both of us had agreed that we would see how exciting it would be to do a lastminute.com challenge and organise it all at the eleventh hour. Why is the eleventh hour such an issue anyway? Are there a lot of deadlines that are exactly twelve hours long? Or maybe twelve noon (or midnight even) is a common time to set cut off times for. Maybe it was coincidence that his text arrived on my phone shortly after 11am.

'Where should we go then?'

I got on google maps at the earliest opportunity and drew an imaginary line between Leighton Buzzard where Harry lived and worked and North East London where I worked and saw what was roughly in the middle.

Hemel Hemstead.

I zoomed in.

And zoomed in again.

I switched to satellite view and looked back and forth a little until I found what I was looking for. And what I was looking for was a pub. Not any old pub, though. It had to be in the countryside, preferably with a large wooded area nearby as woods are good for hiding in. It had to have some footpaths nearby so that we could walk a little way out of civilisation to find a peaceful spot where we wouldn't be stumbled upon in the middle of the night. It had to be close enough to a major road that it wouldn't take me a week to get back to school. It had to have a cool name.

With wonderful village names around Hemel like Jockey End, Trowley Bottom and Flamstead I was literally spoiled for choice. In the end I plumped for Bridens Camp because it sounded in equal parts appropriate and gay. I don't know who Briden is but I don't think his contempories thought he was a man's man, or they did. It's unclear. The Crown and Sceptre looked like a spiffing pub just across the road from the 'Centre of Horseback Combat' which sounds ACE! At first I thought it was the 'Centre of Bareback Combat' which would give it a whole new meaning.

I pulled into the pub car park next to Harry's van. I found him inside already propping up the bar with a couple of pints of cider bubbling furiously in front of him.

'Nice pub,' I commented as he turned to me.

'Nice grub,' he returned using a cardboard menu to gesticulate to the plate of steaming meat and veg that had just been placed down in front of a fellow pub-goer. We ordered briskly and went to drink our pints in the late afternoon sunshine. The sky was clear blue with clumpy white cotton wool clouds lazily drifting across it. The sun cast long shadows and glinted off of Harry's glasses as he squinted towards me. We clinked glasses and chatted about our plans for the evening.

Harry was desperate to do another lip-sync attempt. I was worried that we'd be pigeon holing ourselves into completing these microadventures in a certain fashion. I wanted to try and do as many different things as possible and present our adventures in a range of different ways. Lip-syncing – Been there, done that. Let's move on.

Harry was very persuasive.

'Ok,' I said. 'We'll do one more lip-sync video if you can come up with a decent song.'

'Yeah, but I want to edit the video. So I'll have to record on my phone. We'll have to play the music from your phone.'

Crap. Harry was about to find out what music was on my phone. I tried to explain that I don't really use my phone for music. I tried to explain that my ITunes account had accidentally synced with my wife's. I didn't think I was going to get away with this.

'So what have you got on there,' he asked, a wry smile creeping slowly across his lips, like I imagine a spider would smile like when it has caught an especially juicy fly.

'Um,' I flicked hesitantly thought my music files. 'Adele, Cheryl Cole, One Direction, Taylor Swift, Tina Turner.'

'Sounds like an eleven year old girl's playlist,' he beamed. 'What albums have you got?'

'Glee cast, volume one,' I mumbled.

'Ha,' he snorted into his cider. 'Let's have a look.'

Reluctantly I passed him my phone and he began scrolling. 'Hey, hey. What about this one?' He hit play.

The opening strings of Carly-Rae Jepsen's song 'Call me maybe' started playing at an excessively loud level for a small pub beer garden. A solo drinker on a nearby picnic table raised his eyes from his mobile to glance at the two blokes sitting together. One bespectacled idiot was waving his arms around with a mobile clutched in his hand which had tinny pop music emanating out of it. The other handsome chap cringed and hid behind his fingers. The drinker returned his attention to his phone disinterestedly.

'Turn it off,' I urged through gritted teeth.

Harry just giggled and smirked even wider when the large breasted serving lady came out with two plates of steaming chicken pie and roasties. The buxom barmaid didn't bat an eyelid. She must get camp idiots flailing their arms to teenage pop tunes all the time in her beer garden.

'You're going to make us do a lip-sync microadventure to that song, aren't you?' I capitulated.

'Yep,'

'Bugger.'

Well, if we were going to do this, then I was going to go the whole hog and do it properly. We scoffed our food (while shooting a few verses of the song) nipped back to the car and van to get our gear and started walking down a nearby footpath that Harry had noticed when he pulled in.

It was a wonderful evening. The sun took ages to set so we had a chance to video some footage in actual, real, genuine daylight, which was pretty much unheard of for the last few months. We sang through the song four or five times. One of us held the selfie-stick while the other danced around like a maniac in the background. We swung on fences, chased each other down lanes, jumped up and down in a field (taking special care not to trample any crops), you know the usual stuff you do on a lip-sync microadventure.

We walked for about twenty minutes so that we were a good distance from the pub and tried to find a place that was near a wood but was not in a wood. Why? Because we were going to make a fire!

We strolled off the footpath into an adjacent field. A rough dirt farm track passed between two copses. The copses had broken and disused ground bird feeders, like it had been a game bird pen a couple of years ago but had fallen into disrepair. There was plenty of fallen, dry wood scattered along the floor and hanging from the trees. Firewood would not be a problem. While the light was still with us we did a little collection and soon had a small stack of timber ready to be burnt in a pile by the side of the track. We threw out our roll mats and bivvies on a soft grass verge and relaxed as the sun dipped below the horizon and the stars appeared one by one.

I suddenly realised that I didn't bring the Buxton water bottle that I had in the car. 'Did you bring any water,' I asked H.

'Nope.'

'Bollocks, neither did I.'

'Tell you what, if you go back and get water, I'll get the fire going.'

'Go on then.'

It took forty minutes to walk back to the car, collect the water and marshmallows that I had also forgotten and trek back again. In that time Harry had made a small pyramid of sticks and was blowing uselessly at it.

'Good job, mate,' I said, when I saw his ineffectual attempt. I pulled apart his poorly constructed pyre and rebuilt it just like I was taught in cub scouts, by the pyro kid with the missing eyebrow round the back of the scout hut when Akela wasn't looking. It's a pity I didn't have an aerosol can. That's the traditional firelighting tool of the scout movement as far as my childhood was concerned. After a few persuasive puffs a small flame flickered and the fire was ablaze.

There is something internal, something animalistic about sitting by a naked fire. Especially one you have made and lit yourself. Just sitting and staring at the dancing flames while your eyeballs slowly cook in your head. The flickering fire fairies flit fancifully forwards and f-backwards in your f-vision (Good alliteration Jon!). It's mesmerising and hypnotic and you soon slip into a trancelike state, silence descending on your conversation as both of you are sat marvelling at the magic that is fire. It's very warming both externally on the skin but also internally as the psychological comfort of a fire washes over you.

I don't know if women have these same connections with fire. It's always been seen as such a manly thing to be stood around the barbecue incinerating burgers. Blokes standing round the hot coals at a summer house party are under the same primal urges. Me Make Fire. I Am Man. Maybe it is from the caveman era but surely people have been making fires for years, centuries even. And most of those people have been women, or is that a sexist comment too. I'm trying really hard here not to sound like a bigamist. Do I mean 'bigamist'? Isn't that shagging two people at once? I really need to get myself a dictionary.

We were drawn from our psychic state by a branch burning through in the fire and dropping down to send sparks soaring up into the night sky like fire flies dancing in the smoke. I stoked the fire back up while Harry speared some marshmallows onto twigs. We had a mini war to find the best spot and the best technique for roasting our marshmallows. There is a knack to knowing how close to the flames to put the sugary softness before it catches alight and how long to leave it in there before the gooey mess drooped into the ashes. As was inevitable, more than two marshmallows were sacrificed to the great god of the campfire.

There was no chance of the fire catching anything around it as we'd placed it bang in the middle of the stony farm track. We waited until it had burnt down to a safe level and we retreated to our bivvies, snuggled down into the warmness and gazed up at the stars before we fell fast asleep.

The morning sun rose earlier than we'd been used to and the sky was clear and mild. Harry and I packed our bags in seconds. We were getting good at this camping lark now. We scuffed the last of the ashes to the side of the track and poured our leftover water over anything that looked even a little alive. I took a morning leak on the biggest black log just for good measure. We were strolling back to the car park in under five minutes.

I have to admit that the time it takes to roll up a mat and stuff a bivvy in a bag truly is one of the greatest things about wild camping. Ok, sometimes you have to sleep with a breeze in your face. And sometimes you might get a little bit of drizzle. And the roll mat isn't as soft as your bed. And it can be a bit cold in the middle of the night. And putting on cold shoes in the morning is a drag. But at least you can clear camp in double quick time.

Seriously though, I was really starting to enjoy these midweek adventures. Squeezing a night under the stars into a hectic working week schedule makes you stop and think about your life a little better. It gives you a chance to take a deep breath of clean countryside air and reevaluate your priorities. I don't care what they say at work about me being a lunatic and badger bumming bait. I honestly think the psychological, spiritual even, benefits far outweighs the lack of sleep, the mad dash panic to get back to work on time and the small nagging guilt that I've not done the washing up.

We strolled back to the cars as the morning sun glinted over the treetops throwing warmth and light over the land. We listened to the crows arguing in the trees and saw a rabbit chase across a field. I felt at one with nature and calm and relaxed.

Then I sat on the M25 for two hours in traffic, listening to Oasis on the X-FM. 'My soul slides away'.

June

For the June microadventure, Al had challenged all his acolytes to shoot a creative video, write an epic blog or do something a little bit different for the summer solstice. The day of the year when the night is the shortest and the day the longest seems like the perfect time to get outside for a sleep in the fresh air. As long as you don't mind being woken by sunlight at 4:43am precisely.

Harry's birthday also falls in June and this year he was hitting a big one. That's right. He was turning thirty. Again.

He invited us all round to his parents' house in deepest darkest Wales all the way down in the beautiful coastal county of Pembrokeshire. Known for its Atlantic coast, its historic castles and the Stella Line ferry to Ireland. It's also commonly known as Little England as it's full of expats, which sound like a community of retired Postmen. Many English folk have moved there. I'm not sure why. It's definitely not for the wine, the women or the weather.

Harry parents, the indomitable Mag and the irrepressible Dick, own and run a farm in Pembroke where they make beautiful dairy ice cream. I'm not even saying that because he is paying me. Their ice cream, Upton Farm ice cream, is particularly creamy and lovely. Dick does all the milking while Mag does all the creativity with the flavours. From Strawberry Dream Delight to Butterscotch to the amazingly named Vanilla El Crapino ice cream, which I am reliably informed has 0% crap in it.

What's it like knowing a man called Dick? Well, I'll tell you later if you carry on reading. Deal?

When I said Harry invited us all, I mean he invited my wife, my daughter, our mutual best mate, Greg, who resides in the toxic belch of a city, Newport, Gwent. He'd also invited about thirty of his *other* friends.

Harry is the sort of guy who has *other* friends. Not me, no siree. I've got Harry, I've got Greg and, if she counts, I've got Sally. That's pretty much it. I have work colleagues, yes. I've got people I get on fabulously with, of course. I'm a likeable guy. But other than the three people mentioned here there isn't really anyone else I would drive six hours across the country just to visit for an afternoon.

I've got nothing against Harry's *other* friends. Many of them were my friends too at one stage or another. But friendships for me tend to fall by the wayside unless you put some serious time and effort in to them. And in this day and age who really has the time and effort to put into friendships. I've got about 200 friends on Facebook. Do I go and see any of them on a regular excursion? Do I call them up just to shoot the breeze? Do I heck! Where would there be time in the day to make all those phone calls? Why would I even care?

God I sound depressing.

It was actually quite nice to catch up with some of the uni mates I hadn't seen in a donkey's age. How long do donkey's live for? Ten years? Fifteen years? I'd not seen at least two of them since uni and that was at least nine years ago.

The party was lovely. Dick had put on a great barbecue and all the men gathered around to stare at the burning coals and sip on cold beers.

Due to an administration error, Harry had ended up having two bouncy castles instead of one. He'd ordered one. They delivered the wrong one. It was too small. So they delivered an extra big one as well at no extra cost. Bonus.

Rosie had an ecstatic time bouncing around in the middle of one of them like a giggling rag doll. Harry was his normal effervescent self, bounding between clusters of friends dressed in a big red cape with a giant letter 'H' hanging from his neck on a goldie looking chain, like some sort of super hero gangster (and kudos to you if you picked up on the welsh based rap joke there).

With tractor rides, pass the parcel and a piñata smashing contest the party continued in full swing for many hours and soon it was time for Greg, myself, the wife and the child to leave. Reluctantly I watched as all Harry's *other* friends jumped on quad bikes and in cars and disappeared to the camp ground that was in a nearby field overlooking the estuary. I gave Harry an especially long happy birthday hug, partly to let him know how much he means to me and partly because I hoped that maybe if I stayed very still, Sally and Greg wouldn't notice me and would drive off without me leaving me to continue the fun and whatever other shenanigans Harry had planned for the evening.

All too soon we were back in the Volvo doing a steady 70 back down the M4 in the wrong direction. Away from the fun. Away from the countryside. Away from nature and clean air and whispering winds and laughter and beer and joy and happiness. And back to crappy pukesville Newport, Gwent.

So Harry had a lovely microadventure without me. He slept in a field with all his other friends and had a whale of a time. Or a Wales of a time. Hahaha…. Ahem. Sorry.

I wasn't too bitter about missing Harry's epic party. Well, maybe a bit but I had a much bigger and better plan. Literally the biggest thing I had ever done.

An ULTRAMARATHON!

I had to type that in capitals. I had to do it justice. You have to imagine the bloke off of the X-Factor saying it.

An ULTA-smegging-MARATHON. None of your poxy little every day run of the mill marathons. This one was going to be ULTRA!

Ok. I'll stop with the capital letters. Now.

ULTRAMARATHON!!!

Ok, honestly now. I'll stop.

I'd done the London Marathon twice. The first time because a friend of Harry and mine, who shall remain nameless, because he has no name, challenged us to. Harry and I had both put in for the ballot and been rejected. While Harry was happy to take it as fate's way of saying that marathon running was for fools, I had taken it as an affront and had promptly signed up for a random charity. So after raising the obligatory £2000 and simultaneously emptying my meagre savings and alienating all of my close friends with sponsorship begging (oh, that's why I don't have many close friends. I remember now) I managed to secure a spot on the start line of the marathon.

The run went really well and I finished in under four hours which apparently is quite good. The atmosphere was electric. If you've never run the London marathon I strongly recommend that you do it once in your lifetime.

Whatever you do, don't do it twice.

Two weeks after the first London Marathon I entered the ballot. I was safe in the knowledge that I could tell my entire list of remaining friends that I'd tried to get a place this year but was absolutely gutted that I didn't get through the ballot. Both of them would be really supportive as I quietly cheered the fact that I wouldn't have to do any more ridiculously long runs, early alarm calls, hours creating ingenious ways to raise money for a cause I didn't believe in and countless eons watching myself in a gym mirror going nowhere on a treadmill. Bugger. Maybe I'd enter the ballot again next year.

And then the worst thing happened. I got a place on the London Marathon. Again.

This time it was different though. This time I didn't have the fear that I couldn't do it. I started shirking off the evening runs in the dark and in the rain. I started stopping and walking far more often on the long weekend runs. I'd done 26 miles before. It would be easy.

Come the day of the race and I'd raised a grand total of £10 for charity because raising money is an afterthought when you've raised so much the year before. The race was 6 miles of pure speedy bliss and 20 miles of excruciating agony. At one point I stopped in a tunnel, far from the eyes of the spectators and silently wept to myself as I stretched out a cramping hamstring.

Needless to say I finished in a far slower time. Fifteen minutes slower to be precise and a whole other hour later in other respects.

After that I decided to leave marathon runner to the lunatics who actually enjoyed it.

Three years past and the 2012 finisher t-shirt that I treasured was starting to look very old, almost retro. It'd be like something that Harry might have purchased in Selfridges for £50 claiming it was some sort of bargain.

So when my boss had asked if I fancied doing an ultramarathon (ULTAMARATHON!) I somehow managed to answer in the positive, much to my own surprise.

The ultramarathon (ULTRAMARATHON! Come on now, stop it. It's getting silly) was called 'The Wall' and it was run by a company called 'Rat Race'. 'Rat Race – The Wall' sounds like some insane Channel 5 programme where men dressed as either Wall Street bankers or rats (which could be the same thing, let's be honest) climb the wall from the 90's TV programme 'Gladiators'. Or maybe they're competing in that other TV contest called 'The Wall' where minor celebrities dress up in shiny silver condoms and get pushed into a swimming pool by a progressively aggressive wall.

'The Wall' is really a 69 (oo-er missus!) mile run along the length of Hadrian's Wall from Carlisle on the west coast to Newcastle on the east. The run traverses (apparently) beautiful Northumberland countryside pretty much from coast to coast. It looked epic.

I didn't really know what I had let myself in for. Training started in earnest straight away and my boss, Shane, and I were in the gym three mornings a week and I was putting down some serious mileage at the weekend. This was in October, nine months before the race.

Did I not mention that in between fitting in all the microadventures I'd been training four times a week, sometimes for up to four hours? Are you sure? I'm certain I must have said something.

From Al Humphrey's perspective, this sort of thing is massively encouraged. He is a strong believer in the power of the 'healthy body; healthy mind' mantra and I can't really disagree with him as he is my current idol. I should also support the view from a professional stand point as a PE teacher. Would be a bit silly of me not to advocate doing exercise when I teach it for a living. At least I hope I was being a role model for the kids if nothing else.

Long story short – I did a lot of running, I wore through two pairs of expensive trainers, Sally was pissed at me for spending lots of time away from her and the kid. Ho hum.

The weekend of the race came around and you would have found us on the Friday night trying to work out how we eek more than 60 mph out of the school minibus as we madly dashed up the M6 to get to Carlisle before registration closed. In the van were myself and Shane and three of our colleagues who very kindly had offered to come all the way up to support us. Caroline in particular was particular generous with her time and efforts as neither Barry or Jamie could drive so she would have to do all of the ferrying back and forth between the start and finish line and had even offered to drive the minibus all the way back on the Sunday. Proper ledge!

We registered in the impressive edifice that is Carlisle Castle. While Shane and the rest dully had a massive argument with the people at the Premier Inn who had somehow managed to give their bedrooms away, I slung my rucksack on my back and headed out to a quiet golf course that I had noticed on the map to find a night time sleep spot.

It was weird doing a microadventure alone. A little bit spooky watching every person walk past like they could be a potential rapist or camp site pesterer (Wow. 'Pesterer' is a real word. That's exciting). I found the golf course no problem, spotted a bridge that spanned a river and crossed it, then turned and ducked under it. I'd read on the weather that it was likely to have some drizzle in the night and I thought the bridge might offer a little bit more protection. I felt a little bit like the troll in the 'Three Billy Goats Gruff' story. I probably looked like him too once I'd set up a rudimentary shelter with a tarpaulin and some bungees and snuggled into my sleeping bag.

It is very eerie sleeping on your own under a bridge in a city you have never been to before. All the noises of the tree branches cracking against each other and the odd splash of a nocturnal river creature was amplified in my brain until the whole vicinity was filled with spiky, hairy, scary beasts that were sharpening their fangs ready to devour my prone figure.

After a while I must have dozed off because I was awoken by a couple walking across the bridge in the dark. They couldn't see me, surely.

They didn't see me and don't call me Shirley (thank you 'Aeroplane' for that one!)

Silence, or the sound of night time that is as close to silence as your likely to get when sleeping rough in a Northern city, prevailed and I slept soundly.

I woke to a sky as grey as greyhound, which if you think about it is a stupid name for a dog that is not necessarily grey. It's like heading down to Ladbrokes to put some money on the brownhorses.

I dismantled my makeshift rain cover, which in the end had been unnecessary as it hadn't rained at all, and stuffed all my gear back in my back pack.

Butterflies were dancing the fandango in my stomach. I was super nervous. I'd never even contemplated that I could possibly propel myself 69 miles in one day under my own steam. I might have done it on a bike. Possibly. But how on earth was I going to manage running that distance.

It was at this stage that I started to lament the training sessions that I hadn't been able to commit to due to time constraints and work and family commitments. I'd followed the training regime recommended by the people at Rat Race almost religiously until the distance I needed to run in each of my sessions had become unreasonably long. I was getting to work at 6am so that I could do a quick ten miles before school. I was spending my Saturday mornings, instead of spending time with my family, running to distant towns and villages and getting lost in the countryside. The longest training run I had done was 25 miles from Bishops Stortford to Braintree hoping to catch a bus back in the opposite direction when I had completed the run. I'd run so far that I had outrun the bus service. There were no buses that went that far back east.

My other longest foray had been a walk to work. It was 'Walk to School Week'. A bit like Ronseal it does exactly what it says on the tin and is an initiative at school designed to encourage local students to walk to school. So I decided that I would walk to school on one morning. The only issue for me was that I live about 27 miles from school. I woke at one in the morning to start my trek and spent the next six and a half hours strolling down the towpaths of the rivers Stort and Lea dodging collapsed footpaths, aggressive geese and dodgy canal boat owners. It was actually quite magical as I followed the green swathe of the Lea valley into the industrial congestion of Edmonton. I saw an athletic fox, dozens of ducks and other aquatic birds and even a timid roe deer. I listened to the sweet dawn chorus as the sun broached the horizon. I watched a moorhen leading her chicks for a swim. I chatted happily with early morning dog walkers. It's amazing how un-London-like this small slash of rural Britain is. It really made me feel euphoric. Until I realised I had double year 8s first thing.

25 miles to Brentwood. 27 miles down the Lea Valley. Neither of them would compare to the enormous task of travelling 69 miles. Even if I rammed those two journeys together in one massive walk to work while getting stuck in mid-Essex cocktail then I'd still be…ummmm… take away the 2… about 17 miles short?

I strolled back to the bridge and crossed back over it back towards Carlisle town centre where Shane and the others were holed up in a B&B after being denied a room with the Premier Company. Apparently there was no room at the Inn.

The only people who were out and about at this unearthly hour were a couple of old geezers who were stapling arrows to a post. They looked up at me knowingly.

'You here for the run?' one of them lilted in his northern brogue.

'Yep.'

'Good luck,' said the other as they disappeared down a track like a pair of extremely polite and helpful spirits.

I met Shane in his accommodation and we walked to the castle. The place thronged with luminous people pulling bright macs out of their tiny backpacks as the drizzle started. Some obnoxious person on a megaphone made us line up at the start in the dripping wet as he read through a stupidly long list of health and safety procedures, all of which we had read the night before when we had registered anyway. Big blops of rain dropping from my cap, a small trickle snaking down the back of my shirt and a small cold pool of water forming in each of my running shoes. I blinked through the rain as the starter hooter sounded and we were suddenly swept along in the mass of people out of the gatehouse, across the slippery cobbles and down the road towards Newcastle.

I was massively surprised by how many complete morons were subjecting themselves to such a ridiculous ordeal. I had assumed it would be me, Shane and maybe four or five skinny blokes in lycra. There were perhaps three or four hundred people running with Shane and I. And most of them were over taking us!

We didn't really care. We had our target pace of 5 miles an hour and after my disaster of a London marathon last time we knew the risks of heading off too fast. We'd both agreed that completing the entire race was far more important than doing it in any impressive time. Quite reasonably Shane had pointed out that people wouldn't be even more impressed if we told them that we did it in 20 hour or 22 hours. The pure fact that we had done it would be enough for the vast majority of people.

So we carried on running.

Then walked for a bit.

Then ran a bit more.

Then walked a bit.

Then walked a bit more.

Then did some more walking.

It was probably at this point that we realised that we enjoyed the walking far more than the running and we calculated that we'd still be well ahead of our target.

So we did some more walking.

And walked.

It wasn't really that exciting. We chatted a bit about all sorts of things. We'd both recently become first time fathers in the last year or so. That occupied a lot of our conversations. I also had to put up with Shane banging on about all the romantic stuff he and his wife do together, like random gifts he bought for her or the times she let him go off and do whatever and have dinner on the table for him when he got home. This made me feel equally shamed for not being more spontaneously romantic or thoughtful and gutted that I didn't have a wife who was also considerate and loving. I felt all that Sally did was moan about all the things that I do and all I did was look forward to getting out and doing adventurous stuff. I didn't think our relationship was in a particularly romantic place.

We also spent our time avoiding a complete fruit loop of a woman who was wearing purple spandex and had her hair up in what she thought was ironically quirky bunches but actually made her look like a complete window licker. Her favourite thing to do was overtake us at a gentle jog and just as she was passing let out a massive stinking guff and giggle to us apologetically. I'm sure she was taking a shine to Shane.

Another ancient lady in front of us was steadily jogging in what looked like reverse as we strolled up to her at walking pace. She stopped and walked with us for a while, which actually improved her pace, until she got a bit impatient with all this walking nonsense. She smiled at us, said 'See you later, lads,' and started jogging. We ambled past her and left her for dust.

There were other groups of lads as well. One pair we nicknamed the 'Stop-Starts'. Every time they overtook us at a run they'd stop exhausted maybe a hundred yards in front and walk at a slow pace which enabled us to stomp past them as we rambled on at a sensible steady pace. A few minutes later they'd be back overtaking us again, only for the whole process to repeat itself. It was like they were playing some sick ultramarathon version of leapfrog.

Finally there was Sticky. Everyone wanted to beat Sticky. The 'Stop-Starts' were racing Sticky. Farty McLooneybin was racing Sticky. Slow Po Granny was racing Sticky. Shane and I were racing Sticky. Everyone had to beat Sticky. The reason we all wanted to beat Sticky was because he was cheating.

He had walking sticks.

It's disgusting, isn't it?

He was also bloody quick. And he was only walking. But he was cheating so in the end when he pulled away from us after the halfway station then we didn't feel too bad.

The second half was so much better in some ways and so much worse in others. The sun shone on the beautiful Northumberland countryside. Birds tweeted merrily in the trees. Horses frolicked in the sunshine. Salmon leapt from the rivers. Literally. I saw a salmon jumping up a weir. Incredible!

As we walked through one lazy town called Corbridge and evening pub punters shouted encouragement as they sat in their beer gardens we attempted to arrange our next meeting with Caroline and the boys in the minibus who had met us three or four times throughout the course of the run. The lads had enjoyed spending their down time getting smashed on cheap beer and dozing in sun-drenched parks. Meanwhile Caroline, who had to be stone cold sober to drive the massive transit back and forth along the route, had spent her time creating a progressively more elaborate banner.

Shane was glaring at his phone.

'We'll see them at the next water stop,' he said readjusting his sunglasses on his face and slipping his mobile into a useful pocket on his camelback backpack.

'That's just up this road out of town, isn't it,' I said gazing ahead.

We cantered up the slope with renewed enthusiasm for the promise of Haribo at the water stop and also to dispel the myth that we had walked for the vast majority of this supposed run.

As we turned the corner I saw Caroline with mobile in hand filming our arrival. And then I saw another familiar face. And then another. But these weren't the faces of Barry and Jamie. These faces seemed really out of place stood in this layby in the middle of northern England.

'What the hell are you doing here?' I asked Sally bewildered.

Rosie reached out her stubby little arms for me as Sally and my sister-in-law, Megan stood holding a huge colourful banner. Rosie grasped a small A3 sheet of paper that read 'KEEP GOING DADDY' in large colourful letters. I swung my little girl up into the air and gave her a big hug and a kiss. I was close to tears as I kissed my gleeful wife incredulously.

'What are you doing here?' I repeated.

'We came up to support you.'

'How did you know where to find me?'

'Caroline told us.'

'How long have you been planning this?' I turned to Caroline.

'Months,' she said. 'Finally we don't have to keep the secret.' She glared intently at Barry who held his hands up defensively. I noticed a half finished Coors light grasped in one of them and I ached for a cold beer.

'I've just had to run thirty-five miles without telling you anything about it,' Shane grinned.

I immediately felt ultra-guilty for the feelings of lack of romance in our relationship. Sally had just driven nine hours to come up and stand on a grass verge in the middle of nowhere to wait for her ungrateful husband who was spending even more time away from home and family. What an inconsiderate bastard I am.

'I'm sorry, Sally,' I squeezed her with one arm while I balanced Rosie in the other.

'What for?'

'For not being a good enough husband.'

She laughed it off and smiled at me with loving eyes. How did I bag myself such a great wife?

'You'd better get going,' she said gentling prising herself away from me. 'See you at the finish line.' She took back Rosie who continued to stretch out her arms to me in a desperate attempt to be held. I could still hear her screams as I jogged round the corner and held back a tear.

We walked on. I was full of energy after my encounter with my wife and daughter but Shane was starting to fall apart. While I was eager to push on and at least attempt a jog every now and again Shane flat out refused. It was at this point that he informed me about the lack of cartilage in both his knees. Now, you would have thought that have no cartilage in your knees would predispose you to not do certain activities. Ultramarathons, for example. Hold on a minute. It'd been Shane that had suggested doing an ultra in the first place. Is he actually insane?

So we walked some more. The sun shone at our backs as we walked through dappled forests and across fields filled with flowing grass. We crossed rushing rivers and bubbling brooks. We passed through housing estates, industrial areas, gorgeous country manors and run down caravan sites. We even stopped for an icecream, which was a massive highlight.

As the sun set we were still a long way from Newcastle and we were slowing. Shane's knees had forced us to a mere snail's crawl and we were well below our 5mph target. Unfeeling pedestrians and marshals underestimated the distance to waymarkers which made us second guess our guess of how far we had left to walk and gave unreasonable hope about our speed. These hopes were dully dashed at the next mile marker making us even more demoralised than before. Every unnecessary step was avoided. Every kerb that needed stepping up or puddle that needed skirting was lamented. Every minute extra spent at a water stop was mourned.

I frustrated at our lack of pace. I had to keep reminding myself that it didn't matter that we were walking. We were going to get there long before the cut off time of 24 hours. As the sun eventually disappeared and the sky clouded over all we could see was the pair of small white circles of light from our headtorches as they danced around the trees. I was tired. I was disgruntled. I was bored. I just wanted for it to be over.

Eventually we joined the Tyne at Newcastle and we were on the final straight. Well, straight as a river which bends and turns its way into a major city of the north. We walked along the waterfront where all the night club staff were bidding goodnight to each other. We'd arrived so late that even the nightclubs were shutting. A couple of bouncers gave us a word of encouragement but the warm welcome of clubbers boozily cheering from the various nightspots and the music and lights that would have been blazing across the river were all silent, or asleep, or at the minimum completing the desperate weekend ritual of a hunt for an open kebab van.

We saw the finish line. The Millenium Bridge spans the river like a collapsed wing of a swan. Piercing through the silence was the banshee scream of our fellow work friend, Caroline, as she screamed with foghorn intensity, 'COME ON SHANE AND JON!' She was the other side of the river and had still managed to make herself heard. Definitely a PE teacher.

We looked at each other. 'C'mon, Shane. We can run the last bit.'

Shane grimaced but nodded and we started a slow trundle up and over the bridge.

We crossed the line together, arms raised dejectedly in front of us. Jamie sprayed us with a cheap bottle of bubbly and Barry failed to give us the beer that he had promised us should we have completed the run. We're still waiting for the beer. Our small entourage were there cheering us to the bitter end but there was none of the jubilation of the London Marathon. Being encouraged across the line by five excited friends and family members doesn't even come close to the throngs that line the Mall. I don't want to sound ungrateful. Having five people shouts of motivation being lost in the darkness on the side of the Tyne was better than crossing the line in silence. Our small clan of fans seemed far too enthusiastic for 2 o'clock in the morning and their clamour was a little overwhelming. They made up their lack of numbers with noise and banners and comments they'd been waiting nineteen hours to tell us.

Caroline told us about the crowds of drunk Geordies who'd chased and laughed and celebrated with the runners who finished their race two hours previously. That really made the cramp feel good.

Shane and I bundled into a taxi with the inexhaustible Caroline and we sped off to the local sports centre where a makeshift soup kitchen had been set up on the indoor running track. Shane hobbled off to a table for a massage while I had an excruciatingly slow shower, forced the soup and bread down my neck and waited for Shane to do the same. Looking around I could see maybe a dozen other runners in various stages of disintegration. Some were lying prone on a crash mat under those foil emergency blankets that made them look like roast chickens ready for the oven. Others hobbled back and forth like brain hunting zombies.

One lunatic was attempting to have enthusiastic conversations with people at the soup table. What a moron? Who on earth has energy to have a tête-à-tête at two in the morning having just run 69 miles? Especially with some weird bloke who seemed to still have enough energy to run it again. I just wanted to punch him in his smug enthusiastic face, but I couldn't be bothered to lift my arm.

Caroline, Shane and I eventually got in another taxi that took us to the hotel on the edge of the city where they had booked a room.

Jamie and Barry had gone ahead to check that the room booking actually existed this time so when we arrived Barry's rosy-cheeked face was puffing into a blow up mattress while Jamie was quietly snoring in his own bed.

I grabbed my camping bag from the room and headed straight out of the door. I crossed the dual carriageway that was outside the Travelodge and ducked through a hedge on the other side. I had neither the energy or enthusiasm to find a secluded spot for this bivvy so I threw my roll mat down the other side of the hedge and listened to the cars whizz past on the A-road metres from my head. Just before I closed my eyes I looked up to the horizon and saw the sky lightening as the sun was just thinking about rising.

In the morning the sun rose, as it tends to do. I woke to the cool drizzle of a passing shower which was refreshing as I slowly boiled in the bivvy. I'd never been rained on before on a wild camp. I thought it would be a complete nightmare. It was refreshing and glorious. I can imagine it isn't always like that but that morning, lying in a field with my body inside a warm and dry sleeping bag while delicate summer raindrops sprinkled my face, it was wonderful. In between the brief rain clouds the sky was beautiful blue. The smell of damp hay filled my nostrils and I put my hands behind my head and gazed into the sky peacefully. I realised that I didn't need to get up for another hour and I had done something incredible just the day before. All that busy noise the other side of the hedge was people rushing here and there being busy in their busy lives, oblivious to the care-free camper who was relaxing in the morning sun only metres away in one sense but a million miles in another.

I pulled myself out of the bivvy when I started to get too sweaty to stand it any longer. I strolled across the A-road dodging the traffic and headed to the Subway that was next to the hotel and ordered a foot-long. When it became less of an unsociable hour I went and banged on Shane's door. Barry came bleary eyed to the door. Caroline, in the next room, opened the door, fully dressed with shower completed and hair and makeup in place. I honestly don't know how she does. Jamie was still snoring away.

Caroline recounted the evening's events. Apparently not long after I'd left and they'd all finally got their heads down to sleep a stag party had arrived on their floor. Everything that could go wrong did. At volume. They lost their door key. They slammed the doors. They got caught smoking in their room (why you'd need a fag at three in the morning is beyond me). They refused to leave their room. The police were called. They had a twenty minute argument with the police in the hotel corridor. It got to the point where Caroline had had to get out of bed and shout at them to keep it down.

I was so glad that I had slept outside!

'So, Jon,' said Shane as we eased our aching bodies into the seats on the minibus ready for our journey back home. 'Please can you explain something to me?'

'Sure,' I said.

'Your wife came all the way to Newcastle. She did a nine hour journey in traffic with a baby in the car. She completely surprised you having spent three months planning the whole thing. She did this amazing romantic gesture for you. And when you came to the end of the sixty-nine mile run instead of going back with her to the hotel you decided to sleep in a field.'

'Um… yes,' I agreed suddenly realising the error of my ways.

'If I'd done that to my wife she would have murdered me!'

Here's me on our first microadventure. Is the bottle of gin on the log half empty or half full?

We've just had a dip in the serpentine for at least five seconds, I swear!

Harry's attempt to poison me with raw prawns.

Harry and I tearing into Tenacious D while Rob and his friend attempt to ignore us in the back.

'And all the other boys, try to chase me, but here's my number, so call me maybe.'

Shane and I completing an ULTRAMARATHON!!

Nearly there!

Rosie and her cousins enjoying jumping up and down on our blow up bed. I say our blow up bed but I barely used it.

Look how smiley you are when you wake up in a ruined monastery!

Just a standard days shooting in the woods. I wish

Harry tries to explain the finer points of 'Hooch' during a night of experiments.

Off on my final Christmas urban microadventure.

July

This month was going to be the biggest most organised and most challenging microadventure we had planned for the entire year. It was going to be huge. It was going to be physically exhausting. It was going to be the dream team of Harry and Jon back together again.

But before that happened I had another little microadventure on my own. I'd thought having a solo microadventure would be a nerve-wracking, sleep lacking, poo packing nightmare. It was the complete opposite. It was relaxing. It was stress-free. It was definitely lacking in poo. I could do anything I wanted at my own pace. I mean, doing adventures with Harry are absolutely amazing. Having someone to share all the fears, fun, excitement and endurance with has no comparison. Spending time with your best mate just to shoot the breeze and chat away your worries is cathartic and just something we do far too little of. But having time to yourself where there are no rushes and no priorities and no worries is a whole different form of wonderful.

We had a works night out, specifically organised for a Tuesday night so that I could go all the way out. Due to family commitments Tuesdays were now the only night where I wasn't rushing to collect Rosie from the nursery or from the in-laws.

I decided to follow the traditional parent rule of the free night mash up. The rule is very simple. If you have a night where you are invited out for drinks and you can actually attend (so literally almost never) you drink every alcoholic beverage that is put in front of you. You shun soft drinks as useless stomach filler. You spurn food. Eating, after all, is cheating. You're hungry eyes scan the spirits on the back shelf and the immortal chant of an unleashed parent is yelled at the top of your voice.

'SHO-O-O-O-O-O-O-O-OTS!!'

Quite simply you get so blind drunk that you start vomiting in your own handbag (which has happened to someone very close to me) or attempt to molest a fruit machine because you saw it flashing at you. You get so pissed that you find yourself singing Shaggy's Mr. Bombastic at the top of your voice to a pair of grumpy bouncers in an empty wine bar. 'Mr. Lover lover, a lover, mmmm!'

So I did. I got mashed up. But waking up in the dappled light of a willow tree in a private manicured garden was amazing. I watched a small bird flit about singing merrily in the branches above my head and listened to the peace and quiet of a small secluded spot in the middle of a busy city. I was hidden behind a think fir hedge so knew I wouldn't be disturbed so rolled over and comfortably fell back to sleep. What a great way to wake up after a night out.

I arrived at Harry's pad in Oxford in the early evening on a Friday night. He'd moved to the historic city after his mad break up with his previous girlfriend. He'd moved in with two mates who had kindly lent him a room but he knew it wouldn't be forever as they were being moved out by the landlord the following month. One of Harry's strength is his immensely huge list of people who would just bend over backwards to help him out. He really is such a wonderful guy and he has such a positive impact on so many people that they just would do anything for him.

We checked our gear, climbed in his motor and hit the road. We had a long way to go that evening.

Back in January, after we'd finished our first microadventure when I was infected by the bug bite that Al Humphreys had given me, I'd started making lists of things that I would like to do.

My mum lives in rural Wales up in the mountains in a small village halfway between Cardigan and Carmarthen. On a training run for a previous marathon I had jogged the length of one of the many rivers that lead from the hills to the coast. It had been a fantastic route that had followed the river as it meandered and grew and eventually arrived at the coast. The river had been so inviting as I'd sweated my way along the street. I imagined sitting in a canoe and drifting lazily down the river, all cares thrown to the wind.

This thought revisited my brain as I thumbed through Al's book. Al's 'Source to Sea' microadventure saw him walk and packraft the length of some river in Scotland. A packraft is some sort of inflatable raft that packs down to nothing in your backpack. So it pretty much does what it says it does. Why did I even bother explaining it?

Anyway, these packrafts that Al was raving about. They're bloody expensive. Far cheaper is a blow up canoe, which is what we got.

When it arrived in the post I invited Harry over to look at it. It was massive. There was no way we were going to fit it into a backpack. It also came with two massive paddles. How on earth were we going to transport these?

We put that question to the back of our minds as we spread two Ordinance Survey maps across the floor in the lounge. They covered the area around my mum's house, which annoyingly sat right at the edge of both maps. We traced the snaking blue lines of rivers that ran down from the hills around mum's to see where they popped out on the coast.

Harry followed one particular spring. He carefully followed the line with his finger. He followed it's every curve and bend until he reached the wider blue expanse of the Clennaud. 'I know this place,' he said suddenly looking up from the map with a gleam in his eye.

'Have you been there before?' I asked.

'You could say that,' he grinned. He pointed to a small farm on the map that was by the river he'd been following. 'I grew up on that farm!'

'What, you mean that's your mum and dad's farm?' I asked.

'Yep.' He crossed his arms with a sense of achievement. He hadn't really done anything. Well, I suppose he had been born and then recognised his childhood home from a map. Both were pretty impressive achievements to the novice navigator.

'So,' I said reasoning it through in my head. 'We can follow a river all the way from my mum's house to yours?'

'Yeah. Wow. That sounds really cool. We should definitely do that.' Harry buzzed with excitement.

I should have realised it really. Harry's mum and dad live pretty much directly south of my mum's and mum lives up in the hills while Harry's parents live near the coast in Pembrokeshire. And water run's down hills obvs.

A date was picked in July and we completely forgot about it until the weekend rolled up.

That's a complete lie.

We thought about it loads. We discussed it every time we met. We weighed up different pieces of kit. We contemplated where would be a good place on the river to stop for the night. Where else would be a good place to launch the canoe? How would we distribute the weight of canoe between us? Where exactly should we camp in the mountains? And a whole raft of other questions that go with floating down a river.

Other than that, we completely forgot about it.

We were bombing it down the M4 towards distant Wales. The sun soon set and we were driving through the night, away from the lights and relative safety of the M4 and A4 and off into the darkness of the mountains. Well, hills at least.

The Presellis can be found in West Wales. From the top of them you can see the north and south coasts of the Pembroke peninsular. I know this because I'd reccied the campsite the month before while visiting Mum. I'd persuaded her that a nice walk in the hills was perfect for her, myself and Rosie. What I hadn't told her is that I wanted to sleep rough on one of these peaks.

When Harry and I arrived, it was pitch black. Trying to follow a massive OS map and my vague recollections from my reconnaissance in a wild countryside was difficult. Doing it at night when everything looked completely different with an enormous map that refused to fold the right way was almost impossible. Which is why we got lost. And that's the story I'm sticking with m'lord.

We eventually pulled into the muddy space in the fence line that was mislabelled as a car park spot on the OS map. It definitely didn't warrant a blue 'P' like the one that the cartographers at OS had deigned to give it. It was a layby big enough for one and a half cars to park in in the middle of nowhere.

We unloaded the car and dragged the heavy bags onto our back before trudging up the steep incline in the dark. Harry had offered to take the full weight of the canoe in his bag while I carried both of our sleep gear. It was ludicrous to be carrying an inflatable canoe on a mountain miles from any rivers that would be big enough to launch it in. Not only that but we were walking up hill, further away from the big rivers. Lunacy!

We walked off the beaten track and headed roughly north towards where we could see the springs indicated on the map. The wind was picking up now, just as it had when I had visited the previous month. It had pretty much blown mum, me and Rosie off of the mountain. It was doing the same to me and Harry. This time it was worse though as had the backpacks acting as heavy parachutes, equally unbalancing us with their cumbersome weight and catching the wind to blow us further off course. It was getting difficult to keep our footing. We'd have to find somewhere to shelter from the wind before we put together our small camp.

We found a waist high boulder and made camp behind it. It was past midnight so we looked up to the cloud scattered sky spotting constellations between the blank spaces. We had a long day to look forward to so we tried to get to sleep fairly quickly.

There was a slug on my face.
THERE WAS A SLUG ON MY FACE!!!
What the hell! Al Humphrey never mentioned this in his book. I jerked fully awake in a second, like I'd had a slug slapped in my face. Which I had had.
THERE WAS A SLUG ON MY FACE!!!
I flicked the slimy black bugger into the near distance and rolled myself tighter in my bivvy.

When I woke to my alarm I rolled over on my mini pillow and opened my eyes through the haze of an early morning rude awakening.

He was back. A slime trail trailed, as only a good slime trail can, from the edge of my roll mat all the way to my pillow and up to the large black invertebrate who was insistent on having intercourse with my cheek for the second time that morning. It gives a whole new meaning to the word 'Face-rape'. My work colleagues had been worried about me being bummed by a badger by I was more worried about being sexed up by a slug.

I felt a bit guilty about throwing him out of bed so aggressively earlier in the night so I gently picked him up and placed him on a nearby rock.

I nudged Harry awake and recounted my near-miss and my very clearly not-a-near-miss from the night before. He just laughed.

We stood up from behind our small waist high rock and stretched in the morning sunshine. We glanced up the hill slightly from where we were and saw a massive tor of rocks. A huge ten foot high windbreak. And there was us hiding behind a tiny little boulder. If only we'd walked twenty more metres in the night we'd have stumbled across this edifice and not have to have cowered behind a mere pebble.

We rammed all the camping stuff into my backpack, took a big deep breath of fresh Welsh air and began our journey.

Oh, and Harry had the longest piss known to man. His urine stream sparkled as it arced into the morning light. It was almost beautiful.

We scampered down the hill like two young goats. The morning was wonderful. Red kites glided serenely above us and a couple of sheep skittered through the heather. We followed the lea of the hill looking across to a crevice where the vegetation grew thickly. Here we found a bubbling spring. Water was literally springing from the ground like a plant. Looking down the valley we could see it growing being joined by other springs like a multi tailed snake.

We followed the trickling water down into the basin where it turned into an exciting little stream, then almost instantly into a disappointing bog. Our trainers (which Al had advised me on Twitter would be a good idea) were instantly sodden. We squelched and squerched our way through the swamp. We clambered over a broken gate into an area that had been devoid of grazing sheep. The undergrowth instantly came up to the height of our hips and the unruly tussocks of reeds made every step a gamble of a twisted ankle.

And that was how we walked. At a snail's pace. For four hours.

We dallied with the idea of walking along in the river. Our feet were already drenched from the swamp-like marshland. At least walking in the river we wouldn't get lost. The only problem is that we were going even slower than walking through the swamp. At least walking in the swamp we got the added bonus of seeing wildlife.

Like an adder for example.

Yep, the only venomous snake in the whole of the UK and we only went and found one.

We'd come to another impasse. It was getting difficult to navigate within the river as some inconsiderate farmers had hung barbed wire across the width of it. I don't know why. Maybe to stop intrepid explorers from doing sensible things like walking down the length of it.

We exited the river but found our path blocked by a dry stone wall, which in the saturated conditions we were in really stretched the definition of the word 'dry'. Harry launched his backpack over the wall and scrambled up the loose rocks. As he did so he placed his hand on top of the wall. Inches from a long dull green snake whose black diamond patterned back was infamous.

'Woah,' Harry gasped almost falling from the top of the wall. 'I almost put my hand on a bloody great big snake.'

'You always want to get your hands on a great big snake.'

'No, seriously,' he said.

'Let's have a look.' I chucked my own bag over the wall and climbed up beside my buddy. 'That's an adder,' I said with confidence. 'I've never seen one before but the pattern is unmistakable.' Look at me, the nature expert. 'It's the only venomous snake in the UK.' You knew that already, right?

'Really? Glad I didn't touch it then.'

In all this time the scaly reptile had not even moved a muscle. According to the snake Harry and I really were nothing. It wasn't particularly interested of two members of the most dangerous species on earth. It was such a cool customer, just sunbathing in the morning rays like some slinky babe on an LA beach. We didn't even register on its radar, much like a babe on an LA beach. It was a cold blooded killer, much like a babe on an LA beach.

After our encounter with the adder we enjoyed the company of horses, sheep, butterflies and a particularly adventurous caterpillar who was trying to steal some of our lunch. He was a very hungry caterpillar.

We traipsed endlessly through the swamp and I constantly fretted about the amount of time we had wasted. We were really up against the clock. The trip was designed as a two day expedition with a camp over by the river halfway down where we would toast the fish we'd caught in the stream from the fishing line that I had snuck into a pocket of my backpack. But as the saying goes, time and tide waits for no man and it definitely wasn't playing ball with us. The whole last portion of the river was tidal. There was no way we were going to break our backs trying to paddle against the tide so we had to time our journey with the outgoing tide. The tide times were not in our favour. We'd either have to catch the early afternoon flow or get up at three in the morning (in the rain no less) and paddle in the dark. We opted for the early afternoon option which meant that we really had to get a shift on and this moping about in ankle twisting, drenched to the waist, step-by-step sludge was a waste of time.

When we tumbled over a rusty gate and stumbled across a real road we almost fell to our knees and kissed the tarmac. I sat on a bridge and studied the map while Harry flicked stones into the growing stream below. 'We can follow this national trail that shadows the river,' I pointed out to Harry.

'So we're not going to follow the river?'

'Yeah, we are. The trail roughly follows the river.'

'So we're not going to follow the river?' he repeated.

'No, we're not,' I conceded.

'Is this cheating?'

'Either we follow the trail and catch the tide, or we continue walking at a snail's pace and have to get up ridiculously early tomorrow morning. In the rain.'

'Trail it is then.'

We followed the national trail at a renewed pace. With my incredible navigating skills and Harry's... um... ability to carry a heavy bag, we covered an impressive number of miles in a comparatively short period of time. I resented every uphill as a waste of energy. We were heading down a river and every upward step was effectively a step in the wrong direction. That was one of the beautiful things about walking down a river. It was all down. Well, it should have been anyway.

The sun broke through the grey clouds and beat down relentlessly on our sweaty brows. The bags seemed to grow heavier as we walked dragging us down and making each footfall even more painful. Every time we crossed the river we eyed the depths longingly. We desperately wanted to stop, blow up the canoe and float down the river. Our aching, sweating backs begged us to launch the canoe. 'You two are morons,' our backs screamed at us. 'Just get the boat out already.' But the river wasn't deep enough and we didn't want to get our canoe out too early and end up dragging it through the shallows. We'd be going even slower than we had been during the swamp days. We couldn't afford to slow down.

The national trail we were following was the Landsker Borderlands Trail. It was amazing. The Welsh government must have had some spare cash lying about because the whole trail looked like it had been renovated within the last year but hadn't been used in months. All of the stainless steel gates were brand new but had grass growing through the bars where no one had opened them. All of the boardwalks had shiny unbroken grids neatly stapled to them but weeds growing knee high through the gaps in the beams. All of the signposts were clean cut wood with clear carved and brightly painted

Celtic symbols emblazoned on them but the trees were already starting to claim them back. What a waste of money. I mean I am all for maintaining our country footpaths and national trails but if no one is going to use them, then what is the point? We need to use our rights of way. If we don't we'll lose them. Or worse still, some bureaucrat in a central government somewhere will turn our national trails into some unimportant points scoring, vote securing agenda. Our right to walk where we are free to is far more important than some crappy politician's career.

The national trail also made its way through the middle of two farms. Right through the farm yard. How odd to have strangers constantly walking through your front yard. Seems a bit bonkers to me.

We arrived at the spot next to the river we had originally designated as our camping ground. It was a shallow field where a small B-road crossed the river. We threw our heavy bags down in the long grass and stretched while eyeing the river. The water flowed energetically. We looked at each other and grinned like small children who have found a particularly large sticky chocolate cake. We almost salivated at the thought of not having to carry our backpacks a single step further.

'You reckon?' I asked Harry.

'I reckon,' he said.

We whooped with joy as we dragged the inflatable canoe from Harry's bag and laid it out on the grass. In about ten minutes flat we had the whole thing blown up, pack with the spare bags and floated out on the cool, clear water. Harry wobbled his way into the back seat using the balance skills he had developed whilst sleeping in a hammock. I jumped in the front and we were away.

It wasn't the most comfortable of rides but it was pure bliss. I was sat between Harry's feet and was leant back against big backpack that was wedged down behind my seat. I propped my feet up on the gunwale in front of me. I gently tickled the water with my paddle, watching the tiny whirlpools and ripples as they scattered across the stream. Casually letting a foot dangle in the cold water I turned to watch a couple of coots scoot between some overhanging branches. I turned further back to see the look of innocent glee on Harry's face. He looked like he was having the time of his life but he literally didn't have a clue what he was doing. He was flitting from one side to the other with his paddle and his paddle technique was all wrong. I bit my tongue and turned back to the front.

'Watch out for rocks on the right,' I warned. 'Turn left. More left. Harry, we're going to hit them… too late.'

I turned back to look at him as we had beached ourselves on the rock. 'What?' he said unabashed.

'You realise you are meant to be steering this thing?'

'Am I?'

'Yes. You are in the back seat.' I put my heads in my hands in frustration. How were we ever going to get down this river?

We pinballed from bank to bank like a drunk walking down an alley for the next couple of miles. I swear Harry was aiming for the low hanging branches of all the trees as I constantly had to avoid decapitation on every river bend. After a while he got the hang of it and we actually started to work as an effective team. It came as a shock to both of us.

Out teamwork was really put to the test when we turned a corner in the river and spotted a tree that had collapsed blocking the entire width of the water with a twisting mess of sharp branches and leaves. Being ever conscious of our precious blow-up canoe we assessed the situation. Maybe this was the end of the canoe. Maybe this was as far as we were meant to go. Maybe we'd have to paddle back up river until we found a spot we could jump out.

Not likely! We clambered up the bank using the exposed roots as hand and foot holds. We dragged the canoe up the escarpment and gingerly let it slide down the other side. We relaunched the canoe in the open downstream side of the fallen tree. We were heroes!

I honestly felt amazing after that. We'd faced a complication, a potential spanner in the works but we'd worked together and overcome the situation. I know we were only in the Welsh countryside but we were in the middle of nowhere with no chance of someone coming to save us. We felt like proper adventurers and I felt really proud of the pair of us. Nothing could stop us now.

'Wow. Look at that,' I said a few bends of the river later. 'There's fish jumping out of the river just ahead.'

'Backpaddle! Backpaddle!' urged Harry with urgency.

'Why?' I asked bemused.

'We're about to fall off a weir!'

We both backpaddled frantically until we were out of the rushing draw of the weir. Up on the bank to our left was a water treatment plant and this four foot drop of a weir was obviously some part of the treatment process. Not being an expert on water treatment I can't say exactly how it works. Let's just assume that having two corpses floating in the river after a major canoe related accident might be detrimental to the smooth running of the plant.

We followed a side channel and dropped down a much more appropriate foot high fall and promptly failed to capsize, which was great. Looking back up the river we could see the rushing crashing water of the weir and were quite glad that our mangy little blow-up craft had not had to handle the battering that was sure to have hit it.

The rest of the river was pretty uneventful. It was just chilled out. Lying prone on the back pack with my feet up doing the odd correction paddle here and there just letting the river take me wherever it would was fantastic. The warm sun sneeky peeked through the gaps in the leaves overhead throwing awesome jinks of light off of the little eddies and waves. I could definitely see the perks of canoe travel.

Eventually we turned a corner and an old mill stood grand and dilapidated on the port bank. A great stone arched bridge heralded the end of the standard river and the beginning of the tidal river. Already seaweed strewn roots poking out of dark muddy banks communicated the fact that the tide was long passed turning. We were well behind time. We put the paddle in the water and started to get some sort of rhythm going. It was time to start work again.

The river widened and the mud banks grew. Soon the true bank was some distance away across grey splattered silt where no man dare tread but wading birds quite happily danced up and down. We passed a man and his son who had decided to investigate the river in their own canoe. That's just the sort of thing I'd want to do if I was on holiday in deepest Wales. Something a bit adventurous and a little bit out of the ordinary. Something a bit physical and a bit fun. What a cool dad!

We had arrived at the open river. Now the banks were a hundred metres or so apart and we felt like we were making no progress at all. Each pull of the paddle had the double insult of chucking a handful of cold water down my sleeve and also the undeniable feeling that we were heading nowhere fast. With the oncoming headwind, the aching backs and arms, and the freezing chill that had descended now that the sun had disappeared we both felt really demotivated.

I started shivering. I couldn't control my limbs. I was exhausted and had clearly not had enough to eat all day. We'd originally planned to stop at a pub on the way through but obviously we hadn't had enough time to do that. Harry had been in charge of supplies and had bought nut bars, tracker bars (peanut flavour) and a bag of nuts. He said that he'd read somewhere that nuts are a super food. Well I was super sick of them and hadn't eaten anywhere near enough calories. I was cold and wet and needed to get some layers on.

We pulled onto a solid looking bank and jumped out. We threw our buoyancy aids to one side, each donned an extra layer, slid back into our buoyancy aids and were back on our craft in under a minute.

For the final mile or so we switched places. It was heaven. I didn't have to rely on Harry's dynamic steering technique. I didn't have to relinquish control and resign myself to zig-zagging aimlessly along. Finally I could send our air-filled canoe in an arrow-straight line down the centre of the river.

Isn't 'arrow-straight' a strange term? Ever seen Braveheart or any other period film? The archers always fire their arrows into the air because they know that gravity will bring them down. So an 'arrow-straight' line is a curve. Even Kevin Costner as Robin Hood, Prince of Thieves, had to anticipate the curvature of an arrow's flight, especially in the scene where he shot two horsemen at once, but that was because he'd ripped the feather flights off with his teeth first.

Anyway, we started to warm up and made some serious progress down river.

'Look at the boats,' Harry pointed at one stage.

'What am I looking at?'

'They are all facing downstream now. Earlier they were facing upstream. The tide has turned.'

We had made it to a fork in the river where we needed to turn left, upstream. We had timed it perfectly and the tide gently pushed us up the side river as we paddled the last stretch of our journey. We ground to a halt on the pebble beach on the opposite side of the river to a marina. We both groaned and relaxed our limbs. We had reached the end of the river for us as we had landed on a beach that Harry knew well. We had arrived at the farm. Like a proverbial and literal son, he had returned home.

We dragged our aching carcasses out of the blow-up canoe for the last time and hoisted the canoe, full of all our belongings, onto our heads and portaged the vessel up the small track to the farm. I tried to be enthusiastic but my complete lack of energy denied me any sense of joy or accomplishment. All I wanted to do was sit down and have a cup of tea. We were aching all over, from our shoulders to our calves. It felt like all we'd done is lie down while some ogre had beaten us with our own canoe. It would have been a lot easier if we had been attacked by an ogre.

Finally we got to the end of the farm track, and the end of our journey. Harry's dad, Dick, completely oblivious to our arrival was riding around on his ride-on lawn mower like a new kid on a bike. Harry's mum, Mags, came out to give us both a warm sweaty hug. I mean we were sweaty, not Mags. Harry's Jack Russell pup Pickles came bounding out to greet us with a manically swishing tail. I think Harry's parents got Pickles as an enthusiastic replacement for Harry. Harry tried to be as bounding and energetic but his zest quickly waned.

Mags read our minds. 'Tea?' she asked.

'Yes, please!' we both chorused. We dumped the canoe and head in to collapse on the chairs around the kitchen table.

So that was that. Challenge attempted and completed. There were a few hiccups along the way like a particularly obstructive fallen tree and of course the uncompromising tide times which had a huge impact on how we completed the challenge. But we got there and we were still alive and we had a warm cup of tea inside of us. Well, a cup of tea each. We didn't have to share one mug. Mags and Dick aren't that stingy.

Oh yeah. I was going to tell you why Dick is called Dick.

It was while sat enjoying a small whisky in Dick and Mag's cosy sitting room that I posed the question.

'Dick, why do you call yourself 'Dick' and not 'Richard' or 'Rich'?'

'Yeah, Dad. I've always wondered why,' said Harry who for thirty-one years had never asked his Dad what I thought would be the most obvious question ever.

'Is it because with all the malcs in your family, you would be Tom, Dick and Harry?' I asked as Dick sat there swilling the amber liquid around the inside of his tumbler smiling to himself. Harry's older and sexier brother was called Tom and lived in New Zealand being a doctor doing doctor things.

'That can't be right,' said Harry. 'If that had been the case you would have called me Harry and not Charles Henry.' Yep. Harry is actually called Charlie. Long story.

'Well,' said Dick breaking from his silence and staring us both in the face with sparkling devious eyes. 'The real story starts back when we used to have school visits come to look around the farm. I used to hear the kids snigger and point at me. They'd say to their mates, 'Hey look, that farmer's called Dick!' And I thought it was so amusing that I continued calling myself Dick every time the school kids visited. And then I started calling myself Dick with everyone. It's really funny to see people's reactions.' Trust Harry's dad to spend a lifetime doing one long practical joke.

'Is that it?' said Harry. 'I thought there was some great big reason and you just did it for a laugh?'

'Yep,' said Dick leaning back in his voluptuous armchair ginning.

'Makes sense,' said Harry who could be the only one to see sense in this bizarre excuse for calling yourself a male appendage. 'My last girlfriend refused to call you Dick. She always called you Richard.'

'Which is one of the reason I never liked her,' he finished staring intently into his whisky like he was going to improve the flavour with the power of the Force. He drained the last drops and declared that he was heading to bed. We followed behind shortly after.

August

A few weeks later Sally's dad, Sean, came to stay. He and his buddy, Red, were flying out of Stansted airport early the next morning and so were using my house as a stop gap between home and the airport. I got home from work and found the pair of them propping up the bar of the Irish pub in town. Sean is a short in statue but large in persona and is always the centre of attention. He was holding court with the Irish barman. Red, I assume, used to own a crop of red hair but is, alas, sporting hair as white as a sheet of paper. He was trying to keep up with Sean's incessant banter. They were well into their drinking session and both insisted on buying a round, which I then had to reciprocate. Three pints in on a work night while these two drunks had a minimum of five under their belts made the walk home a tediously long one (Wow, squeezed four numbers into that sentence. Ha! There's another one). When we got in I put Red up in my bed, as in I showed him where it was, I didn't physically force a man I barely knew into bed. That would just be wrong. Sean took the spare room.

'You'll be sleeping on the sofa, so you will,' said Sean in an excessively thick Irish accent. Thicker than normal to show off to Red or because he'd been chatting to the Cork landlord, I wasn't sure.

'Nope. I'll be sleeping outside tonight.'

'What'll you be doing that for?' he asked confused.

'It's going to be a beautiful clear night, not a drop of rain, and warm as well. I think I'll have a kip down on the lawn.'

'Don't be silly, now. You can have the bed if it means that much to you.'

'No worries, I'll be grand.' Crap, now I was putting on an Irish accent.

'See you in the morning,' he bade good night and closed the door.

I snuggled down in my sleeping bag and gazed up at the sky. It wasn't great, if you ask me. Most of the stars were just not strong enough to compete with the orange glow of the streetlights of surburbia. There was no refreshing cool wind as I was in the middle of my garden shielded by six foot fences on all sides. The air was thick and mild and the lawn was firm under my roll mat. I rolled over and tried to get some sleep.

At four in the morning Sean called out to me, 'Jon, will you sort us out a taxi?'

I watched the birds flit between the branches of the eucalyptus tree at the bottom of the garden with an energy that I just couldn't comprehend, let alone muster. I squeezed myself out of my cosy, warm bivvy, slipped on the trainers that I had left by my side and trudged into the house.

Sean was busy making himself and Red a tea and bemoaning the lack of Barry's teabags. I found a number for a taxi on my phone and rang it. On my smart device. Which Sean also had a version of in his pocket. Why did I have to get up to ring him a cab?

'Taxi will be here in five minutes,' I mumbled as I head towards the stairs.

'Are you not going back outside, Jon?' Sean asked looking up from his steaming mug.

'Nope, I'm going to bed. Have a nice flight.' I waved over my shoulder and went and lay on the bed upstairs, fully clothed. I listened for the sound of the front door being carefully closed, the slam of two car doors and the rev of an engine before I rolled over and went back to sleep.

I've come to the conclusion that doing a microadventure in your garden is crap. Yes, it's easy if the weather turns bad but that is the problem. It is too easy to get out of there. The lure of a comfy double bed with a soft mattress and a warm duvet is just too much at five in the morning when the chill has set in. On all the other microadventures there had been no option, no escape to the land of luxury, aka indoors. You were there and you braved it out til the morning. That is what an adventure is, going through something difficult but coming out of the other side feeling really good about yourself for having done it. And all the outdoor stuff as well, of course.

Also, my lawn is really bloody hard!

Sally, Rosie and I were off on our own holiday. We'd booked a cottage in Devon with plans to visit the beach and eat ice creams and go for bike rides and all the other stuff that families do on holiday.

Before we would be sunning ourselves on the soft sands of Saunton admiring the Atlantic coast, we had to visit my mum in Wales. She was having her now annual (if it happens twice in two years, that makes it annual, right?) big family barbecue. My step-dad, Colin, had invested in an automated spit-roast machine from Germany. It was the height of efficiency in engineering and my mouth was already drooling in anticipation as we drove down the M4 to sunny Wales.

I was pootling along minding my own business giggling along to Jack Dee and co. on 'Sorry I Haven't a Clue' on Radio 4 when who should pull in front of my Volvo but my brother, Rob (remember him? Back in April. You do? Fantastic!), who was also driving home from London that evening. Such a bizarre coincidence. We drove in convoy the rest of the way, stopping for the obligatory race out of the blocks at the Severn Bridge toll booths. I hope you do that too. The moment the barrier lifts everyone in the car screams as I slam my foot on the pedal. I don't know who I'm racing. It could be a lorry. It could be an old biddy in her stationwagon. It doesn't matter. I lean my head forward to increase the aerodynamics. I switch gear with split second timing. I'm always the first to the finish line, which is the point where the three lanes re-merge. Next time you are at the booths and you see the bar start to raise have a quick look left and right. Maybe I'll be racing you!

Anyway, we arrived at Mum's smallholding well after dark. And by dark, I mean dark. There is virtually no light pollution at Mum's. This was the complete opposite to my and Rob's microadventure to Southend. Literally, the other side of the country. Where Southend had been glowing orange overcast, which had been beautiful in its own way, this was the complete awe inspiring mesmerising grandeur that was the clear night sky. The stars were so bright and clear and there were so many of them. We could identify individual stars and constellations in all their glory. We could see smudges of nebulas and other galaxies. We could see to the end of time.

A shooting star flew across the sky. I felt like I was in a Steven Spielberg movie. Then I remembered that it was the Perseid shower and I'd already been told all about this by Al on his blog.

The maddest thing about staring at the mind-blowingly amazing night sky on such a clear night with practically zero light pollution is that this is pretty much what our ancestors saw every night. No wonder so many of our myths and ancient religions involve the spectacular vision that I had before me. I was literally looking at heaven. I suppose that's where the word 'staring' comes from, people gazing enthralled by pinpricks of light from the deepest reaches of space.

We bundled into the sleepy house, gave Mum, who'd been waiting up for us, a big hug, and fell into bed.

The next morning we woke to find my youngest and maddest brother, Ted, attempting to heat a blow up swimming pool with a metal bin full of fire. No, I have no idea how he was going to do it either. Colin was extolling the amazing mechanical genius that was his spit-roaster while Mum was simultaneously complaining about the amount of dirt and studiously avoiding doing any cleaning whatsoever. Rob was in the barn arranging bowls of food on a table with my step-sister, Esther. My eldest brother, Anthony, would arrive with his brood later that morning and my step-brother would be thundering up the drive on his monster bike later that day too.

And if you think that is a large family, you'll be pleased to know that there's more. The middle brother of our five, Tom, was in Australia on the first leg of a round the world adventure. He's doing one of those, see-how-long-my-money-lasts types of adventure. His gallivanting around the world letting the wind take him where it will makes my paltry camping in the garden adventures look a bit poo. I'm not the least bit jealous, honest.

We also had a plethora of family friends and aunts and grandparents visiting for the barbecue. Can you have a plethora or family friends? Maybe a gaggle would be a more appropriate collective noun. It made for a noisy, exciting but relaxed and chilled sunny barbecue at the farm.

What a lovely idyllic picture you paint of a family gathering, you might be saying, but what on God's green earth has this got to do with microadventures? Hold your horses, I'm getting to that bit.

So, my main job of the morning, while the organised chaos of the feast preparations was in full force around me, was to erect a tent.

Yes.

I know.

A tent.

It's hardly wild camping, is it? I'm paraphrasing Al here but 'Camping is a crap version of sleeping indoors'. And he was right. Camping in a tent is now as abhorrent to me as child molestation. Not that child molestation was at any point ok by me. Maybe that wasn't the best analogy.

This microadventure was going to be a bit different. You may have noticed that there is a certain lack of mention of a bespectacled, mop-haired moron this month, and that is because Harry was off doing his own microadventure, which I will get on to. This particular microadventure marked a milestone in a certain little person's life. Not only was it going to be Sally's first microadventure, but it was going to be Rosie's first camp EVER!

It must be amazing being young doing loads of 'First Evers' pretty much every day. Sally's got a photo album somewhere. 'First Ever Smile'. 'First Ever Bath.' 'First Ever Fart.' It's a book of memories for a baby that will have no memory of it but it is something that I hope she carries for the rest of her life. 'First Ever Skydive.' 'First Ever Circumnavigation of the World.' 'First Ever Woman on the Moon.' Can you imagine a life full of 'First Evers'?

As microadventures go, and camping to be fair, we'd be in the relative luxury of a four-man tent, with a blow up airbed, duvet, sheet and pillows. We even managed to squeeze Rosie's travel cot into the sleeping quarters. It wasn't quite 'glamping' but I couldn't hold my hand on my heart and say it was real camping either. Not without retching at least.

The barbecue went swimmingly, especially when Ted managed to hook the burning bin up to the swimming pool water pump via an ingenious system of bent copper pipes. The stars came out for a second night's display and the hardcore few who still remained sat around a bonfire drinking shots and playing Cards Against Humanity. Even the legend that is my Grandad joined us in the drinking games until he said it was time to hit the hay. Not literally. I mean we were in front of a barn full of the stuff but he had a perfectly respectable bed to return to.

Sally and I stumbled drunkenly into our tent and were soon snoring Zzzs into the midnight air.

Of course it woke the baby and she spent the rest of the night hogging the airbed while Sally and I tried to fight her for the duvet.

My backside, which had been denied any sort of feathered cover, was freezing while Rosie lay peacefully snuggled in the bed clothes.

Harry's adventure was a whole different kettle of fish. And by that I don't mean that instead of a spit-roasted leg of lamb he had decided to boil mackerel in his kitchen appliances.

On the same night that I had a frozen butt after being booted out of my blow-up bed by my belligerent offspring, Harry was holed up on a hilltop on Lundy island.

Hal had gone back to the farm for an adventure, and adventure he had had. After hitching a ride on Dick's boat, they'd sailed out from the Pembroke peninsula to the distant headland of Lundy. After disembarking onto the island he'd spent a night in a churchyard overlooking the cliffs with the cry of seagulls and the crashing of waves as his lullaby.

When morning came the waves had been too rough for Dick to bring the boat close to land so Harry had been abandoned to find his own way home. He'd approached the ferry company who'd begrudgingly sold them a one-way ticket back to the mainland. I say begrudgingly because there should be no such thing as a one-way ticket as camping on Lundy is strictly prohibited. How did this loony get to the island? Where had he stayed? The mind boggles.

Now a ferry ticket off an island is great, if you end up going back to the same country from which you sailed. Harry's ticket, however, was for Ilfracombe in Devon. He then had to hightail it via bus and train, via Barnstaple, Exeter, Bristol, Cardiff and finally Carmarthen, where he was met by a humbled Dick in his Land Rover. He'd done the whole journey wearing nothing but the clothes he stood up in and carrying nothing but his camping gear.

As microadventures go, it was an extreme one. The danger of illicit bivvying. The dilemma of the route home being compromised by poor weather. The endeavour to find a solution. The grit and determination (and cost and monotony) to travel the distance by various means of transport. The jubilation of finally getting home. The story to be told to friends afterwards. It made camping in my Mum's field in a tent under a duvet seem a bit pathetic.

Not that I'm comparing the two.

I'm not competitive. Honest.

September

For our September microadventure Harry and I decided to team back up again. Partly so that we could share our adventures, partly so that Harry didn't go off and have another incredible adventure without me.

We thought we'd latch onto Al's idea about getting a whole load of friends together and going out for a bivvy all in a group. Maybe a bonfire on a hill. Maybe some shared whisky. Who knows? We thought that September would be a good time before it got too dark and cold at night for the uninitiated to join us on a camp out.

Harry had been kicked out of his house that he had been sharing with his mates a few months before (no fault of his own, he says, though I reckon it's because he's far too loud) and had since moved into a room in a house in the centre of Oxford. He was desperate to show off the sights and sounds of the city to his *other* friends so he created a Facebook event and the ball was rolling.

I say *other* friends but in this instance it's a bit harsh. One of the lads had been invited to my wedding, another of the girls was in the same digs at uni as Sally, one of the lads lived across the road from me and Harry in first year so it wasn't like I didn't know these people. Some of them I'd not seen since I'd left uni almost ten years ago so it was going to be great to catch up.

'A Bunch of Punts' Harry had named the Facebook event obviously intending us to hire an armada of crafts when we eventually all found each other on the bank of the river Ox on a sunny afternoon.

'Hilarious,' I'd told Harry after giving one friend an awkward hug and kiss and another a manly handshake.

He was completely in his element, jumping from punt to punt swinging his pole in the air. 'Jon, stop being such a punt,' he had just said with a huge grin on his cheeky face.

He galloped to the back of one of the boats and shoved his pole into the mud. 'Last one to the pub buys the first round,' he yelled over his shoulder and then drove his small craft and its unfortunate occupants into an overhanging tree.

Pete looked across at the calamity Harry was causing and called up to me, 'I'm glad I'm in the boat with you!'

I guided our vessel with smooth elegant pushes and gentle guiding rudder strokes and we whizzed past the stranded boat. The screams of frustration and Harry's defensive cries were soon long in the distance as we floated up the river. It was such a beautiful day. The sun was playing peek-a-boo behind fluffy white clouds. A pair of swans swam effortlessly near the bank. A cool breeze tickled the water into excitement. And I lay my head against the pole and chatted amiably with the passengers on my boat.

Pete had been one of our terrible four in first year. That's not a name we called ourselves. We didn't really have a team name. Maybe we should have been the Fantastic Four. I think Marvel might have had some words to say about that.

The other member of our 'team' was Mike. He'd had enough of London life so had followed the exotic lifestyle and tax breaks to Hong Kong.

Pete had been on the same management course as Harry at university and for some reason had decided to befriend him. They are nothing alike. Harry is a four-eyed geek. A loud extrovert with a mad dress sense. Pete is Mr. Cool. Good looking and relaxed. One of those strong silent types. Fit as a school of dolphins and just as sleek. He shaved all his body hair off. Not for fun or to be more like a dolphin but to streamline himself. He was a triathlete, you see.

I have literally no idea why he wanted to hang out with me, Mike or Harry.

In a mirror of my life, Pete had married a girl from House 16. Hattie was tall, elegant, blonde with a sharp wit. She'd been head hunted for the university rowing team and she show-jumped for a hobby. She was living how the other half live.

It was Hayley who'd I'd not seen since uni but after floating down the river with her and Pete for the last twenty minutes I had come to the conclusion that they were exactly the same. Pete was a little bit hairier where he'd given up the triathlon but that was about it.

It makes you think. Do people ever really change or are we pretty much who we are going to be for the rest of our lives?

And after the 'Sex in the City' esque conundrum let's get back to the river where Harry had finally mastered the art of steering a punt.

'Do you know what?' Harry shouted as he snaked up the river. 'Doing that paddling in the back of the blow up canoe has definitely improved my punting.' Watching him bounce from bank to bank I could see what he meant. I had scary flashbacks of getting a faceful of branches and scraping across rocks in the middle of rapids. I manoeuvred my punt out of Harry's careering path and we both pointed upstream to the pub.

We landed the craft, enjoyed a slap up lunch in the beer garden overlooking the river and glared enviously at the carefree kids rolling down the grassy hill nearby. Oh, how I would love to throw off the shackles of maturedom and throw myself into a log roll down the incline. The kids giggling laughter taunted me.

It was nice to catch up with old friends. Alex, an extraordinarily wary man, was sat with his long term girlfriend (now wife) Anna. They are a wonderful pair of people and Amy has this miraculous power over Alex by making him not be a bit of a prat, which is good.

Also at the meal was Nathan and his girlfriend Allie, who in an 'it's-a-small-world' kind of way, was house mates with my brother-in-law at uni and works in the same office as Sally. Although I know Nathan mainly as Harry and Alex's friend, he also happened to live in my house which I vacated in third year. Things are very incestualised at the University of Bath.

Suffice to say there was a good group of us, all of which knew each other pretty well.

We de-punted and strolled through town until we eventually made our way to Harry's pad, where his freaky housemate was dominating the kitchen. She stared at us with gleaming beady eyes from above a cauldron of boiling bats blood cackling maniacally.

Sorry. Got a bit carried away there. Harry's just got a housemate who's a bit odd. She was in the kitchen stirring a saucepan with pasta sauce in it. And she didn't cackle. She just looked up at us annoyed for having nine tipsy idiots invade her quiet household. She humphed and stamped upstairs with her ravioli.

We took the hint and soon headed out for dinner. We crossed a bridge, headed through a gate and suddenly we were on a common with lowing cattle and a river running through it. How many other cities in the world do you turn a corner and have cows chewing the cud on a pasture? Cambridge, maybe.

We were walking along the river when Harry turned to me. 'Jon,' he said suspiciously.

'What?' I answered cautiously.

'Fancy a swim.' His eyes sparkled mischievously.

Now we had been planning to do a wild swim on pretty much every microadventure so far. Other than a dip in the Serpentine, which we can all pretty much agree was the worst excuse of a microadventure so far, we hadn't been able to scrape together the courage to immerse ourselves in anything other than a good book ('Moods of Future Joys' / ''Thunder and Sunshine' – Cheers Al!).

This time it was different. This time it was a warm summer's day. The sun had been beating down since after lunch when the fluffy cumulonimbus had drifted off to lands afar and the warm dead air was calling for us to take a dip.

I looked at Harry.

He looked at me.

We grinned at each other like naughty school boys.

'Let's do it!' I cheered.

We dropped our trousers and threw off our shirts in about three seconds flat. Without dithering or giving our brains a chance to have a second, probably sensible, thought we ran into the shallow river.

The water was colder than it looked. I kept running with cool water splashing up my legs, then dived head first under the surface.

I popped up spluttering for breath as the chilly water sapped the oxygen from my lungs. 'It's bloody cold,' I squeaked to the floppy haired head that bobbed next to me.

'It's alright once you get moving.'

I heeded his words and started an awkward breast stroke towards the opposite bank. Within moments I had warmed up. Either that or I had become too numb to notice the cold. I laughed and splashed Harry. He splashed me back. It very almost turned into a scene from Dirty Dancing. The feeling of the water was wonderfully refreshing after the warm depressing heat of the afternoon. The fact that I'd been able to do something childish and silly made up for the inability to roll down the grassy hill with the kids at lunch time. How does the phrase go? 'Growing old is mandatory. Growing up is optional'. I was loving doing something really stupid, invigorating. Something that makes you feel alive again on a hot afternoon.

That was until I put my foot down into the wet oozy mud. The gross feeling as the cow pat / silt mixture squelched between my toes.

I know it was a cow pat / silt mixture because a cow was watching me with disinterested eyes from the bank. We were busy swimming in her drinking water.

I grimaced and turned back towards Harry to protest at the disgustingness of it all. Just as I did I noticed the vanishing figures of Alex and Nathan as they ran off with our clothes from where we'd left them by the footpath. They were laughing hysterically. It wasn't funny!

We pootled around in the river for a few more minutes until the novelty of swimming in what probably amounted to heavily diluted bovine urine wore off. We scrambled to the bank where thankfully Alex and Nathan had come to their senses and returned our clothes for us. They had, however, neglected to return Harry's trousers and were holding them hostage somewhere.

'I have a spare pair of tracksuit bottoms in my back pack,' I told Harry happily.

'Why?'

'I have literally no idea.'

'Thanks,' he said with a mixture of gratitude and confusion. 'Now, don't look because I've got to get rid of these boxers and after swimming in that cold river I don't think I'm going to impress anyone.' And he didn't. He especially didn't impress the river cruise that chose that exact moment to go past. The ladies having finger sandwiches washed down with tall glasses of bubbly were particularly unimpressed, though you couldn't tell by the way they pointed and laughed.

Getting naked in public once again. This was starting to become a bit of a habit.

We both went commando and shoved the wet pants in side pockets of our bags. I found mine a few weeks later and they still smelled of river. And wee. In some ways I hope it was cow wee. In others, I hope it wasn't.

We joined the rest of the group at the pub where Harry had booked a table. We stood around the bar while we waited for them to set our table laughing at our escapades in the river. The others, i.e. everyone apart from Harry and myself, thought it was lunacy.

Why strip off and jump in a dirty river?

In the middle of the day.

In a public place.

On the way to the restaurant.

Harry being the ever caring hygiene freak insisted we go and wash our hands before dinner.

Alex, laughed and pointed at Harry. 'You found your trousers then? No. Wait. Those aren't your trousers?!'

'No,' I said. 'I had a spare pair.'

'Why?'

'I have literally no idea.'

'But I hung your trousers on the gate as you come into the restaurant,' Alex said confused. 'Didn't you see them?'

'Nope,' Harry and I said in unison.

'I bet someone has nicked them,' Alex said, suddenly sounding like his normal angst self.

'I told you not to leave them there,' said Alex's girlfriend, Anna.

'But they couldn't have not seen them when they came in.'

'No buts. You'll have to go back and get them.'

'But…'

'What did I say?'

Alex took a mournful slug of his pint, gave me and Harry a dirty look and traipsed out the back door to the gate by the river.

'That's Karma for you,' I said smiling.

Harry was soon reunited with his trousers and we all sat down to a lovely dinner. I had a beautiful steak with a dark currant sauce. I can still remember the tang of the berries with the juiciness of the rare steak. Yummy. Yummy. In my tummy.

'So, who's camping out with us tonight?' I asked between mouthfuls of succulent meat.

'We're staying at Harry's,' said Alex, motioning to Anna, Nathan and Allie with his fork.

'We're heading home after this,' said Pete.

'What?' I was perplexed. 'I thought we were all camping out with a bonfire on a hill. I thought we were going to share whisky. I've been practising 'Kumbaya' on the guitar.'

'Jon, we don't have a guitar,' pointed out Harry unhelpfully.

'That's not the point.'

'I'm still coming,' said Harry.

'At least *you* are up for camping out. Not like these losers!'

Alex just laughed at my sulky attitude.

The meal finished and we said goodnight as we all went our separate ways at the river. Dusk had truly set in. The sky was clear but the moon wasn't up and when the light quickly faded from the sky, so did our visibility. We fished around in our back packs for our head-torches.

We'd walked a little way down the river and Harry had disappeared into a hedge to find some dry wood for the camp fire.

'I've found this,' said Harry emerging from the copse with a ten foot tree over his shoulder.

Harry took us to a ruined monastery that sat beside the river. As the night air cooled a bank of fog drifted over the water and wrapped the tumbled down walls in a soft eerie grey blanket. It was super spooky. We snuck into the ruined compound via a gap in the dun coloured sandstone wall and headed for the only free standing structure in the apparently large grass covered courtyard. I say apparently because our torch beams wouldn't reach the far side of the clearing due to the thick mist.

We ducked into the building which looked as if it had been the chapel. Inside we were protected from the chill air by four walls and it was noticeably warmer. It was even toastier when we got a small fire going in the middle of the floor and watched as the smoke and burning embers danced up into the ceilingless sky.

It was glorious, just lying there watching the flames cavort in between the twigs and the half burnt tree that Harry insisted on dropping on the fire. 'I've carried it this far. I'm going to watch it burn,' he reasoned. We barely shared a word as we sat in peaceful tranquillity snuggled into our bivvies around the toasty warmness grilling marshmallows on the end of a pointy stick.

This is what bivvying is really about.

Honestly, I bitch and moan about being cold and not being adventurous enough but to just sit and be still for one or two moments in this hectic world of ours, to just spend a moment with ourselves not really thinking but just being. That is what wild camping is really about.

'Ow! Ow! Ow! I can'b geb ib off!' I yelped.

'What's wrong?' Harry turned to me concerned.

'I've go' burnin' mar'mallow shtuck to ma top lip!'

Eventually the fire died down as I lay gazing up at the dark sky above. It was as if I was lying in the great hall in Hogwarts and someone had bewitched the ceiling. The gentle warmth from the low flames kept my body and face toasty as I closed my eyes to sleep.

Suddenly I heard it. Footsteps along the path by the edge of the monastery. I lay there listening to each crunch along the gravel. They were coming nearer. I was conscious of the remaining light from the fire that was illuminating the inside walls of the chapel and would be visible through the mist through the pane-less windows. If we were discovered now, it would be anything but painless.

The unknown pedestrian crunched closer to the outside wall of the chapel and then stopped.

I held my breath, not that it would have done anything. Reducing the oxygen travelling into one's body has not been proven as an effective fire extinguisher. I waited as the seconds ticked by. What was the stranger doing? Who were they? Were they someone official who had come to give us a bollocking? Were they a local who had a vested interest in maintaining the peace? Were they a monastic fan who'd just come to investigate a random ruined monastery in the middle of the night? I waited to find out.

I never did. The footsteps eventually continued along the path until the sound had completely gone. I couldn't sleep straight away. I had a lot of unanswered questions. I had half a mind to get out of my bivvy and chase this intruder down to find out exactly what he'd been doing disturbing our sleep. That half of the mind didn't win the argument and I snuggled deeper in my bivvy and slowly drifted off.

October

Harry has a friend called Boat Bob.

Boat Bob lived on a boat.

You probably guessed that.

Boat Bob doesn't live on a boat any more but he will forever be known as Boat Bob.

Interestingly Harry used to live on the boat too but Harry has never been called Boat Harry as far as I am aware. Maybe he is to Bob's mates.

I hadn't seen Boat Bob for years as he is one of Harry's *other* friends. And as one of Harry's *other* friends Boat Bob was invited to Harry's birthday party back in June. You remember that one. The one with the double bouncy castle fiasco.

Anyway, at that party Boat Bob and I had got talking and Boat Bob had told me that he had heard about these microadventures that Harry and I had been on and he really wanted to get involved. Like, really badly.

You see, Boat Bob was now married with a kid, which is one of the main reason why he doesn't still live on a boat. Being married with a kid doesn't exclude you from living on boats. It's just not recommended by netmums (this has not been corroborated with netmums!).

Also, being married with a kid doesn't exclude you from microadventures, as I think I have proven over the last nine months. So the fact that he wanted to get involved, like, really badly, was something that I wanted to help with as much as possible. If I could facilitate just one more micro-dad-venturer then I think this whole year long debacle has been worthwhile.

I sent him a group text.

We got a date in the diary.

It was a Monday, which for me was a massive push. I'd have to drive Rosie to the in-laws in Buckinghamshire, bath her, feed her and put her to bed, then wait with uncontrollable anticipation for Sally to get back from London after work. It relied on a whole load of cogs falling in to place perfectly.

Rosie was bathed.

She was fed.

She was in bed.

I was sat twiddling my thumbs, checking my watch every thirty seconds. I sent another group text to confirm the meet time and place.

Bob text back.

'Sorry to let you down lads but I won't be able to make it.'

What?

You're kidding right!

I'd bent over backwards to help a fellow dad become a micro-dad-venturer. I'd organised baby cover and had driven halfway round the M25 to make sure it all worked.

And he'd just text, that evening, that he couldn't make it.

I rang Harry.

'What's going on?'

'I know. It's very unlike Bob. I'll ring him.'

I stood looking out of the window watching the trees blow in the darkness. What a waste of my time. Why had I bothered getting everything in place only to be let down at the last minute? Did people not realise that this wasn't just something I did whenever I felt like it. Every microadventure was planned in minutiae. Well. Sort of. Each microadventure had required Sally to be put out to enable me to go off gallivanting around the country doing daft things and sleeping in stupid places. And now this microadventure was being pulled out from under my feet.

My phone buzzed in my hand. Harry's name was on the screen. 'Yep,' I answered curtly.

'He says he can't make it and he's really sorry.'

'Right,' I said through gritted teeth.

'Do you still want to go on a microadventure?' he asked.

'Nope,' I said. 'Bye.'

You may think this is a bit of an overreaction. I mean, yes he'd cancelled last minute, and yes I'd put myself out. But surely that'd be even more reason to do the microadventure. To be honest, I just wasn't feeling it. We'd missed all of daylight. It was going to be a return to microadventures in the depressing darkness. I'd had a really long day at work, not to mention the really long drive in ridiculous traffic just to get to where I was. I'd put people out left, right and centre and was feeling guilty for that as well. All in all, I was not in the mood to sit in the darkness outside in a random wood somewhere.

And it had started raining.

None of that mattered though. What really mattered was that this was the third time that Boat Bob had bailed on us. He'd been so enthusiastic at Harry's party in June but now I was offering him a microadventure on a plate he wasn't interested. I felt like I had been led up the garden path. I felt like I'd been invited out to dinner, I'd ordered and paid for an expensive bottle of wine, and then been stood up like a douchebag.

A microadventure would have been perfect for Boat Bob. He'd been 'stuck' with his family thinking about how his life was not what it was and now he was just too frightened to take the first step. As Alastair says, taking the first step is always the hardest. Harry and I had tried to make his initial foray into the world of microadventure as exciting and painless as possible. We'd selected a date that was good for him. We'd bought extra kit so that he could take part. We'd planned the wild camp to be near him. We'd done everything but he'd still bottled it.

In the end though I had to take a philosophical position. Maybe, even with all their bravado about lost youth and the lamentation of missing adventure, maybe, just maybe, some people like their lives the way they are. Sans l'adventure.

I don't get that at all.

I got a call from Harry.

'Jon, don't get too excited but…'

I love when he starts a sentence like that. That's the sort of prefix that you know is going to be followed by something amazing. I was already grinning and nodding.

Fast forward one week and I'm sprinting through King's Cross station with a small rucksack packed with a change of clothes and my camping gear.

It's a Thursday lunchtime. I'm always amazed at the sort of people who are just walking around on a Thursday in the middle of the day. What do people do for a job if they have time to just walk around on a work day afternoon? Are any of them rushing to a mad adventure?

Kindly my work colleagues had said that they'd cover my lessons that afternoon. I'd taught a double year 8 lesson period one and two and dashed out of the door and across the capital to catch a train to Oxford.

I was sweating when I threw myself in my seat and tore open the Cornish pasty I had managed to grab in my frantic haste. I'd made it. I relaxed and slowly chewed the pastry covered meat and veg. The train rocketed through the countryside frightening flocks of crows from a field. A small herd of deer raised their heads to watch me pass. I felt easy and calm watching this idyllic rural landscape fly past the window but equally thrilled with anticipation for the excitement and fun that I knew I was rushing towards.

Rewind one week and Harry was finishing his sentence.

'Jon, don't get too excited but there's a chance that someone wants to make a TV programme about our microadventures.'

'Wow, really? That's amazing!' I said, clearly holding my excitement in.

'It's only a maybe. I've been approached by an American production company who are looking at making an adventure food programme.'

'Sort of like Bear Grylls meets Heston Blumenthal.'

'Exactly,' he said. 'Basically, they took the idea to an American travel TV company and they said that they liked the idea but they thought it'd be even better if I did it with my mates.'

'That's brilliant.'

'Yeah, so I've invited my mate, Tommy, to be in it. You know Tommy, right?'

Harry had mentioned Tommy a lot. He lived in Georgia in USA. He flew planes, drove speed boats and camped out at every opportunity he could. He was a proper adventurer.

'Yeah, you've mentioned him once or twice.'

'So I said that I wanted to involve you. I know it'd be difficult for you. I know that you'd have work and Rosie. Please don't feel you have to do it but it'd be amazing if you can be in it too.'

I thought for about it for about three seconds.

'Yes!' I said.

There comes a few moments in life when you just need to say 'Yes'. Sometimes in life you have to move heaven and earth to say

'Yes' but that 'Yes' is the right answer. It's the only answer. I have found that I have never regretted saying 'Yes'. I look back on my life and realise that the times I wished I had, the things I'd turned down, the occasions that I'd said 'No', these were the moments in life that I most regret. Sometimes it just takes a little bit of bottle and a pair of melon sized cahones but if you just said 'Yes'… Just imagine where your life would be now.

(Ever read 'YesMan' by Danny Wallace. I spent a whole year devoted to this book and its message. Don't watch the Jim Carrey film. It's crap.)

Yes. YES. YES!!!!

Fast forward all the tedious emails back and forth organising the logistics and I've been picked up at the station by the two person production team and dumped unceremoniously in a car park in a wood near Oxford.

Tommy is another bespectacled, tall chap but he's far more reserved that I expected. I thought he'd be loud and obnoxious like Harry but he ended up being charming and introverted and sardonic. We got on brilliantly immediately.

While Tommy was busy filming an exciting car chase scene (ok, he was just pulling into the car park) in a baby blue VW campervan, I got changed and Harry fretted about his apparatus.

I've mentioned that Harry is a food entrepreneur. What that basically means is that he makes ridiculous food inventions and then markets them as essential party fodder at la-di-da corporate dos. He started off with his liquid nitrogen ice cream buggy where he'd make wonderfully smooth ice cream in front of your eyes. He's progressed on to edible mist machines and candy floss canons since and he's always got some wacky invention in the pipeline.

What he was worried about today was that he wouldn't be able to produce enough dry ice from a fire extinguisher. Standard Harry.

After three or four takes, Tommy climbed out of the campervan and the director / camera operator came over. 'Hi, has Harry filled you in on what is going on.'

'Not really,' I replied.

'We're shooting a taster today. We're going to put together some clips to show to the production company what the show might be like. Hopefully we can get some good stuff.'

'We've been down at the river all morning,' added Harry gesturing to Tommy and himself. 'We "collected" pure salt from a river.' Harry did the finger quote thing when he said 'collected'.

'Wow. How did you manage that?' I asked.

'We sent Tommy out to the middle of the river in a blow up canoe. We siphoned some water onto a plastic sheet on the bank. Using the power of the sun's rays we were able to evaporate the water off the plastic sheet leaving only river salt behind.'

'That's amazing,' I said, genuinely impressed by Harry's scientific know how. 'I can't believe that worked.'

'It didn't. We just threw some table salt onto the plastic sheet.'

'Right.' Of course. The magic of television.

'So what we are doing now,' interjected the director, 'is shooting the morning scene. The river is in the afternoon and the mud salt is in the morning.' Again the magic of television where morning is afternoon, afternoon is morning and a monkey's your uncle.

Wait.

What?

'Mud salt?' I asked.

'Yeah,' said Harry grinning. 'We're going to make salt from mud!'

'Ok,' Tommy and I chorused.

I was quickly micced up by the two production girls who seemed to have far more clue what was going on than the director. We all climbed in the van and jumped out again and started the shoot.

I've decided that shooting a TV programme is dead simple. I'd even go so far as to say that editing the same TV show is fairly simple if you have the right shots and the right tools. I've also decided that I was a far better director than this woman was. She had no idea what was going on, couldn't link one scene to the next or see how it fitted into the overall picture. She had no concept of time or light or narrative. But I learnt a lot watching her. My only wish was that I could have a piece of kit as decent as she was lugging around all afternoon. Her camera was very impressive.

A quad bike riding warden for the woods screeched to a stop in the car park just as we were about to start filming a new shot and demanded to know what we were doing. We definitely looked dodgy with a bag of camping gear and cooking utensils thrown over each of our shoulders.

'You know you can't camp here, right?'

The production girls helped relieve his concern, which sounds more enjoyable than just telling him that we weren't camping (which we were pretending to do). Or making a fire (which I planned to do). Or committing trespass (which I'm pretty sure we were already doing).

Harry, Tommy and I lugged our gear down into the woods while being trailed by the director, and further back by the two production girls.

Their job seemed a cushty one. Standing around gossiping. Chatting to local park wardens. Playing Clash of Clans on their phones. Seemed a right doss.

We found a clearing in the woods that looked like a badger's sett. Upturned earth mounds surrounded deep holes. 'This will be perfect,' said Harry. 'The mud that's been dug up should be easier to get the salt from.'

We filmed shots of us throwing our kit down. Shots of Harry explaining crap. The same shot again and again. We tried to be spontaneous but when the director changed angle and told us to 'Just say what you just said,' it wasn't helpful. We couldn't remember what we'd just said.

Harry extracted an electric probe from his rucksack and Tommy, using his degree in Astrophysics (he's adventurous and super smart. I'm sure he was being perfect just to highlight how crap an adventurer I was), determined where the best spot to dig was. The higher the electric current the more salt was in the ground.

I pointed out that the nearer the electrode were to each other the higher the current too so we did a bit of television magic and found a spot that was 'naturally' high in salt. (What a load of bollocks!)

I was finally useful and dug a hole. That is literally the extent of my skills. On this adventure, Tommy had been the driver, the scientist, the sarcastic comedian. I dug a hole. Wow. Look at me go.

Harry held aloft the sod of earth that I had removed from the poor badger's roof and I licked it. I'd be damned if Tommy was going to be more outrageous than me as well. It tasted of dirt. Actually, that's what I said to camera. It didn't taste of anything. It was just a bit gritty. Like a mouthful of sand rather than a mouthful of compost. Not that I've eaten either.

We put the soil in some water to dilute it and then tried to filter it through a piece of kitchen roll. A super absorbent piece of kitchen roll. One that didn't let a drop of liquid through. That is until we broke the kitchen roll and then our nice clean measuring jug was filled with pale yellowy brown muddy water. Was I going to have to drink this?

Harry set up a stove. But he'd run out of gas. So we faked evaporating the muddy liquid. Oh, the power of the magic of television.

Suddenly, as if by some wizardry we had a wok (yes, THE wok from our adventure in March) full of crystalline white table salt, er, I mean mud salt. We each dipped our finger in and tasted the salt and through amazing acting skills portrayed the fact that the table salt / mud salt tasted like dirt. I think we need Oscars.

Not long after Harry and I sat on a log talking to the director who stood behind the now tripodded (that's clearly not a word!) camera smiling benignly as she listened to us drivel on about our adventures together. We worked out that the biggest adventure we had been on together was the canoe adventure that summer. It seemed strange to us that despite everything we had been through over the last few years together, and there were a whole load of stupid misadventures and scrapes we had been through, there were almost no adventures abroad. We'd both been on our own travels. Me to Thailand, Kenya and the US. Harry to India, China and Canada. But we'd only been abroad once together and that was to Disneyland Paris. How were we going to persuade an American travel company to invest money and resources on a couple of idiot Brits who'd barely been off of their own shores together? How could we show that we were both adventurers destined for greatness?

I massively struggled in this interview. The director insisted that we direct our conversation, outbursts and sound bites at her and not the camera lens. This was despite not looking at us at all but watching the whole thing through the eye piece of the camera. I don't know what she was looking at. She'd already set up the shot.

She also insisted that I call Harry, Charlie. This was Harry's fault to be fair. Everyone knows him as Harry, unless you know him professionally, in which case he's Charlie. It's not some Superman alter ego. Don't expect Harry to step into a phone box, remove his glasses and step out claiming to be from Krypton. No. Harry is just spineless. It all started back in his first placement at uni… (cue wibbly lines that denote thinking back to times past)… wibbly… wibbly…

Harry was on his first placement in London at some swanky ad agency. He had arrived at the offices to find this jobsworth of a lady holding a clipboard calling out the names of the newly arrived placement students. I imagine her like a Nazi lieutenant during roll call at a prisoner of war camp but I do have an overactive imagination!

'Charles Francis!' she'd bellowed in what I can only assume was a German accent.

'Hi,' said Harry like the awkward nineteen year old English P.O.W. that he was. 'Uh, is it alright if you call me Harry.'

'No! Zis iz not ok. It sez here zat you are Charles Henry Francis. You will be called Charles or Charlie only.'

'Oh. Ok,' He'd replied timidly. Oh, how he would live to regret it.

So throughout his professional life and even when he started up his own company Harry was known as Charlie. It has now got to the point that you know how long people have been friends with him for based on what they call him. I particularly love calling up Lick Me I'm Delicious headquarters. 'Can I speak to Harry please?'

'Um, there's no one by that name working here.'

'Ok, in which case, tell Charlie he's a bellend!'

'I'll pass you over.'

I've never met Rhys or Jake but they seem like top blokes.

Where was I? Oh, yes. Harry, Tommy and I travelled back to the baby blue campervan that had been sat forlornly in the car park. Now the real fun was going to begin.

'The reason we want to find salt,' said Harry to Tommy and myself and to the black cyclops eye that was the camera lens, 'is so that we can make the perfect tequila slammer!'

Now you're talking, I thought. I'd caught the train so I could have a drink or two. This was going to be ace.

We all clambered into the van where Harry had set up his edible mist machine. What he hadn't done is remember the correct lead for the machine so it couldn't be plugged in. Once someone had found a lead that could be plugged in to the car cigarette lighter hole thingy we realised that that too couldn't be used as it wouldn't fit either car. So no mist machine, but no problem. We had the power of the magic of television.

He'd managed to make a small amount of dry ice which he threw into the machine so it started smoking. The lights weren't working but no problem.

'Throw the salt in there, Jon,' he said.

I did my best throwing salt acting. I was immense. Film offers would soon be flying in.

'So if we suck in the mist, neck our shots and suck our lemons we've got a tequila slammer made with pure river salt.' Course we have, Harry. Now pass me another tequila.

I was wobbling after the first three takes. Tommy and Harry were both driving so it was up to me to finish their shots for them. What a way to be spending a Thursday afternoon.

Then it came to the final shot of the day. This was the big one. This shot was the one which would stick in the minds of the TV people. This was the shot that would seal the deal.

'So what's the plan?' asked the clueless director.

'The plan was to have a wide shot of the van filled with mist from the machine with all the lights from the mist machine flashing.'

'And can we do that?'

'No. The mist machine isn't working.'

'So what are we going to do?'

'Tommy's going to let off a fire extinguisher.'

'Great.'

'It's not entirely safe.'

'Oh.'

The director and the production girls moved off a distance. The sun had just started turning the sky a bright burnt orange and we were twenty minutes from being locked in the car park. We had one fire extinguisher and one chance. It was now or never.

Harry, Tommy and I clambered back in the van. I was a bit bleary eyed at this point and can't remember how it happened but I managed to knock over the entire water filled mist machine contraption sending a cascade of fluid all over the inside of the van.

'At least we're sending it back to them clean,' Harry reasoned.

Finally, after much squeegeeing with left over kitchen towel, we were all back in and ready for the final shot. We sat and waited for our cue.

When we heard the director call, Tommy let rip. The campervan instantly filled with carbon dioxide gas as the extinguisher belched its fumes. Everything was enveloped in a cloud of white. I battled to hold my breath. Suddenly there was silence as the extinguisher became extinguished. A surreal tranquil silence fell over the van. I knew Harry was less than a metre in front of me but I couldn't even see my own hand in front of my face in this custard-thick CO_2 fog. I could hear my heart beat thumping on my ears like I was stood outside of a drum and bass rave in my own head. My lungs screamed for oxygen as we sat there awaiting the call for cut from the director or for the cloud of fumes to dissipate.

Neither came.

I couldn't take it anymore and slammed open the door of the campervan and sucked in beautiful, precious oxygen.

'Does anyone feel lightheaded?' asked Harry nonchalantly.

'I feel oxygen deprived,' I said.

'Didn't you breathe?'

'What? Pure Carbon Dioxide? I don't think so.'

'Oh, it was perfectly fine to breathe normally. You just might have felt a little light headed afterwards, that's all.'

So I'd almost died of self-asphyxiation for no reason. That would have been interesting to explain to the wood warden as he trundled up the road on his quad bike. 'Don't worry mate. We didn't camp in your woods but we did manage to suffocate one of our talent.'

By the way, that's what we were called. The Talent. Ha! What a joke this all was. Stood with heaving lungs next to a food genius and a bone-fide astrophysicist pilot adventurer I felt about as far from talented as the entire England rugby union squad at the recent World Cup. I was such a lame arse.

The director wasn't entirely happy with the final shot but there wasn't much we could do about it. Thanks to Harry's amazing planning skills we'd run out of ingenious ways to make the supposed 'salt-mist' that we were meant to be inhaling. The mist-machine wasn't working. The fire extinguishers were all spent. We had no gas for the camping stove. Dusk was falling and the light was failing us and the woods were closing in six minutes. The film crew would have deal with the final shot in post-production. Look at me with the technical jargon. I'm telling you. This directing lark is a piece of cake.

We hastily threw everything in the vans and cars and skidded out of the car park.

Other than a few final shots of us all in the baby blue VW campervan bombing it down country roads that was pretty much it. I was invited out for dinner with Harry and the crew but declined as I had a long journey ahead and a daughter to take to nursery in the morning. Not to mention work on a tequila slammer hangover.

I was dropped at the station in Oxford and caught the returning train back to London. The night sky was already dark and the agricultural landscape that so inspired me on the way out of the city was dully disguised behind a tired and bedraggled reflection of my own face.

I was already thinking about all the ways I would have done the filming if I'd been the director. Having made almost ten videos about microadventures over previous months I was getting to be a bit of pro. Maybe, Harry, Tommy and I could make the TV show ourselves. We didn't need a flashy film crew and production assistants who stood around updating their Facebook profiles. Maybe I should invest in a jazzy new camera to get better quality shots. Maybe. Maybe.

A few weeks later I got sent a link by Harry under the express conditions that I didn't share it with anyone as it was still technically 'owned' by the production company. I clicked the link.

The video was professional, I'll give them that. But what amazed me and made me feel awesome about my own filming skills was that they'd nicked loads of shots from our previous microadventure videos. My shots of Harry jumping rivers, stepping through gorse bushes, climbing into a canoe, all taken from mad angles with interesting compositions and they were all mine. The editor had decided that my shots of adventure were superior to the material that the director had filmed with us in the woods.

Told you I was better and she was crap.

Not that I'm competitive you understand.

November

I have a mate from rugby called Smiler. He's the sort of bloke that you just look at him and you know he plays rugby. He has a face like a warthog that's run into the back of a bus. His nose has broken more times than Del Boy's Reliant Regal van. Or maybe that should be Trigger's broom. His ears are the sort of cauliflower that you'd expect from a heavyweight boxer. His thickly furrowed brow could compete with Gordon Ramsay's. Or a gorilla's. Basically, he's not the sort of face that you'd want to see in a dark alley.

He has, however, got the most amazing twinkling eyes and a grin that connects both his ears together. He is just the most caring individual who will move mountains to help out a mate. He's one of those blokes who have the most amazing listening skills. You'd go to the pub to have a conversation and realise that you've unloaded you're whole life to him and haven't even asked him how his day has been. That's not me being inconsiderate. It's just the way Smiler controls the conversation.

Quite simply he is a top bloke and I'd be honoured to call him a friend. Personally I don't think I deserve that title. Mainly because Smiler invites me out for a drink pretty much every week and I have to turn him down on every occasion because of family or microadventure commitments.

So when he invited me to his brother's stag do, I jumped at the chance to attempt to reward some of the loyalty and friendship that Smiler had sent my way.

I also thought I was doing him a favour. Smiler had sent a group message to a whole load of the rugby club inviting them to the stag for his brother, Jamie, despite the fact that Jamie doesn't even play for the rugby team. It seemed a little bit desperate, so I thought I'd help him out by making up numbers.

When I arrived at the designated pub late one Friday evening I found all four of the party sat around a table having a big plate of pub grub each. Yep, four of them. That was it. There was Smiler, Jamie and two other gents that I had never clapped eyes on before in my life. They were also all old geezers. With my arrival I think I had brought the average age down by about ten years. They gave a half-hearted cheer when I walked in and quickly returned to their food.

Bugger this, I thought and headed to the bar. 'Five flaming Sambucas, please,' I asked the barman.

I carried the lit liquid carefully back to the table. One of the two fellas, the slighter of the two with less hair immediately stated, 'What the hell is that? I'm not touching any shots!'

No shots?! On a stag do!

Inexplicably this guy's name was Loon. Inexplicably because no one explained to me why he had such a name and also inexplicably because there was nothing at all 'Loon'-like about his persona or attitude. I found him a grumpy old sod who refused to have any engagement with the activities for fear of 'getting a bit drunk with all your rugby drinking games'.

The other lad, tubbier with a tightly controlled mop of black hair on his head, had a much more sensible name of Mark. This guy was more my cup of tea. As the evening progressed and the alcohol had loosened his tongue, I found out that he was a director for an open water swimming lake in Norfolk as well as having swum the channel once before. Here was a fellow adventurer. Here was a kindred spirit.

Speaking of spirits, shot roulette (5 shots, all red, lucky dip to see what you get) was well underway when best-man Smiler brought out his piece-de-resistance. He'd made a wheel of fortune (or wheel of misfortune – which is what Harry made for my stag do a few years ago). Where the pointer stopped, that was what we had to do. Some zones said to drink certain amounts of your beverage. Some stations said to nominate other people to drink. One station, the one that the pointer always seemed to fall on, said simply 'Eggstrordinary'.

The first time it fell on 'Eggstrordinary' I turned to Smiler and said, 'What's this then?'

He already had his infamous cheeky glint in his eye as he beckoned me to the back door of the pub. He led the small gaggle of half-pissed blokes into the beer garden. It was then that I noticed the box of eggs that he had carried out with him and placed on a garden bench. 'Jon, you stand over there.' He pointed to one end of the flood light patch of grass. 'Mark, you stand over there.' Mark moved to the other side of the small lawn. 'Now, all you've got to do is catch an egg. You've got three tries.'

It was a mild autumnal evening and the grass was slick with moisture. I positioned myself at my designated spot and watched as Mark carefully selected his weapon of choice and took aim. The first egg went flying over my head and smashed into a tree at the back. The second was a better throw but skidded past me on the grass unscathed. The third I made a real effort to catch. It's not that easy catching eggs in the half light of a floodlit beer garden. The egg I reached for exploded down my arm and splattered my sleeve in gooey mess.

Well, that was fun, I thought to myself. Now I'm covered in ovum. Delightful.

After that we hit the drinking games pretty hard. The barman had some old Essex drinking dice game that came in a box. I'm not sure of the name of it but essentially you rolled a dice and flicked down number blocks of wood on the box until, hopefully, you managed to shut the box. Hold on. I think that's the name of the game. I think it was 'Shut the Box' but don't quote me on that because I was starting to feel a little worse for wear at this point.

Traditionally, as in way back when it used to happen fairly regularly, when I am on a night out I have this switch inside my head that suddenly engages when I reach a certain level of drunkenness. It's one step before becoming paralytic and one step beyond making sensible, rational decisions. When this trip-switch goes, I'm gone. Whatever pub I'm in, wherever the night club is, whoever I am with I suddenly think, right that's it, and walk out of the pub and make my way home. I usually have no idea how I manage it. I like to think that I am part homing pigeon. Whatever the reason I always manage to make it home to bed.

This of course is all a distant memory now that I am a father!

On this occasion it was a bit different, though. On this occasion I'd be camping out. Smiler had invited me into his tent with Jamie and Mark (Loon had long ago disappeared to his caravan with his wife). I declined, informing them that I had my own sleeping arrangements organised.

I stumbled back to my car, extracted my bivvy from the boot, threw it down in the field at the back of the pub and was asleep in moments.

I'm telling you, if I had the option this is how I would end every night out ever. It's brilliant! You sleep like a log (which I would have done regardless with the skinful of booze that I had). You are getting fresh air all night which can do nothing but aid in your hangover. You can literally sleep right outside the public house that you have just frequented. And there's the added bonus that if you need to vomit in the middle of the night all you have to do is roll over until you are clear of your roll mat and hurl to your heart's content.

Idyllic.

I'd been bored one evening in my kitchen and was flicking through my Facebook while waiting for some pasta to cook. I suddenly fell upon a video.

'Life hacks'

I clicked on it and watched it. Very clever, I thought. I wonder if there are life hacks for camping.

There were loads of them. Video after video. I watch life hacks on starting fires, on opening tins of tuna, on cooking steaks. Recipes for Smores, how to break apart a battery, how to make a camping stove from four tent pegs. Video after video.

The pasta burnt. Sally was not impressed.

After putting a fresh pot on and assuring Sally that this time I would consider the neighbours should the smoke alarm go off a second time, I started to make a list.

I wrote down things that Harry and I could do together. Things that involved minimum kit but would be maximum fun and excitement. I texted Harry and we soon had a date in the diary.

Tuesday, because it had to be Tuesdays now as that was the only night Rosie would be at the in-laws, came round soon enough and I jumped in the car after work and scooted round the M25 to High Wycombe.

The place where we were going to be camping was less than ten minutes drive from where my wife and child would be spending the night but while they were lying cuddled up in a massive double bed and a cot respectively, I'd be bedding down with a much stranger fellow.

As usual, I found him propping up the bar in a pub, ordering a pint. He had a menu in his hand and he was running his finger down the main courses.

'Hi, Harry,' I said.

'Heya, mate. I was just about to order,' he smiled brightly.

'Scampi and chips,' I said barely glancing at the menu just to check that this usual pub fare was on there.

I have this test. It's called the 'Scampi and Chips Test'. It's really simple. If it's my first visit to a pub, more often than not I'll have the scampi and chips. If it's good, then it's probably a pub that I'll visit again. If it's not than that particular public house has lost my patronage. A lot can be said about a pub by its scampi and chips.

'Fair enough,' Harry murmured. He placed his order and we took our pints to a table.

'Mad weather tonight,' I said after supping my cider.

'This wind is crazy,' he agreed.

'It's meant to be 60 mile an hour winds tonight.'

'Crazy. So, what's the plan?'

'We're going to do a whole load of experiments. I've seen a ton of 'Life Hack' videos on YouTube so I thought we could put some of them to a real life test. I thought it would be something that you might include in your travel / food programme that you might be doing. Do you want to know what experiments we're going to do?'

'No, no,' he said raising a hand defensively. 'I want to find out as we go along.'

'So where did you pick to camp?' I asked him. I'd picked the general area but Harry had been in charge of finding a place we could pitch.

He pulled his phone from his pocket. 'I really want to camp here,' he said swooshing his fingers over the screen until they had zoomed in on a very clear and obvious structure.

'Do you think that's a good idea?' I asked. 'Won't it technically be trespassing?'

'*Technically* all wild camping is trespassing.'

'Good point.'

Yep, wild camping is technically trespassing in the whole of England and Wales (but interestingly not in Scotland where there is a right to roam. Wales are also thinking of going down this route, which I personally can't do anything but indorse). Theoretically we would need the permission of every land owner for every piece of ground that we camped on. Realistically that ain't gonna happen. Al views it in a positive way. Wild camping is accepted mainly because you arrive after everyone has gone to bed and leave before anyone gets up.

As long as you leave no trace then no one is bothered, or even finds out.

We finished our pints and shovelled the hot meals into our gobs before calling our thanks to the beleaguered bar staff and heading out the door. If you were interested, the scampi was overcooked and the chips weren't chunky. Not a good omen for a revisit.

A little way down the road we came upon a country track that lead up a hill into a wood. 'This is it,' said Harry as he started up the track.

It was properly scary. The woods heaved and moaned as the high gusty winds buffeted and crashed into them. The trees groaned and protested and gave up as the sound of crashing branches could be heard through the rustling roar of the trees. The air around us was weirdly calm as we sought the shelter of the trees but the moment were we out the other side in an open field the gusts caught us and flapped out clothing and battered our bags. Leaves bashed across the long grass like lost souls in a storm. It had the feeling of danger despite just being air rushing between areas of different pressure. I was glad Harry was with me because I think I would have retreated back to the car if I'd been alone.

We skirted the woods and carried on up the hill until we saw the eerie white silhouette of our destination in front of us.

The manor house was sheaved in darkness but the light sandstone walls made it stand out from the night like a ghost of a house hovering a few feet off the floor. From where we were stood looking up the length of the lawn it looked like it was on a raised pedestal as the manicured lawns and flower beds acted as a visual elevation for the main building itself. We leapt a fence and were soon in the grounds of the country house.

'We are definitely trespassing,' I said looking around worried.

'Don't worry, Jon,' said Harry breezily. 'If anyone asks you can just show them your National Trust card.' Yep, like that was a good excuse in to be camping on their lawn in the middle of a blustery autumnal night.

We ducked below the lea of the raised lawn and found a relatively flat piece of gravel footpath that was as far out of the wind as we could manage. 'This'll do,' I said. 'Did you bring your camping stove?'

He pulled the collapsible blue stove from his rucksack and laid it in the middle of the path.

'We're going to light your stove,' I said pausing for dramatic effect. The storm blowing around us helped with this a bit. '…with this!' I held aloft a small AA battery.

I explained how if you tore apart a piece of tin foil in a certain way you could connect it to both ends of the battery and the resulting heat should light a piece of kindling. For kindling I had a pack of Doritos crisps which when crunched into a cheesy powder makes a high fat lighting material.

I don't know what was wrong with my tin foil tearing technique but it wasn't working.

We tried again.

And again.

We ate the crisps and tried one more time.

It didn't work.

Experiment number 1 – Can you start a fire with a battery?

Answer – not in 60 mph winds!

'Well, that was rubbish,' said Harry.

The next experiment involved making our own candle wax by melting down some mayonnaise over our gas stove. I started to spoon the Helman's into the mess tin when I noticed the pale blue label.

'I think we're going to have a problem with this experiment,' I said.

'Why's that?'

'Well, we're meant to be separating the fat off of the mayonnaise to use as our candle wax.'

'Right, so. What's the problem?'

'I've accidentally bought low-fat mayonnaise.'

'You idiot,' he laughed.

Experiment number 2 – Can you make candle wax from mayonnaise?

Answer – not from low fat mayonnaise.

This was going downhill fast.

'The next experiment is to make a candle using an orange.'

'Ok.'

'So I scoop out all of the juicy orange flesh and leave the pithy stuff behind to act as the wick.'

'Oh that's clever.'

'But we don't have any candle wax to put in the candle.'

'Shall we just eat the orange?' he asked helpfully.

'Let's just eat the orange.' We split the orange in half, scooped out the inside of one just for good measure and ate the juicy innards.

Experiment 3 – Can you make an orange into a candle?

Answer – not without candle wax.

The discarded half of orange sat mournfully on the ground by the stove. It was an empty vessel waiting to be filled, like its whole role in life had been smashed by people who insist on buying low-fat mayonnaise. I mean, why does it even exist? If you want mayonnaise you should be forced to eat the proper stuff. It's not like the low-fat stuff even tastes like the real stuff. It's like Diet Coke as well. Tastes nothing like real Coke. If you don't want the flavour of Coke and you want to drink something that has zero sugar in it, then have a bloody glass of water and stop filling our supermarket shelves with your no-fat, no-sugar, zero-caffeine rubbish. It's all a massive con by the food and drink companies and as soon as people work that out the sooner we can all go back to worry about real things like world poverty and terrorism.

Pepsi Max, on the other hand, is far superior in flavour to regular Pepsi.

'Did you bring a belt?'

'No, today I'm in slacks,' he said as he pinged the waistband of his elasticated jogging bottoms.

'Brilliant.'

'Why?'

'I was going to use your belt to open these two bottles of Hooch.'

'What the hell is Hooch?'

'You've never heard of Hooch?' I then preceded to recount to Harry the many times as a teenager getting older kids to buy me the sickly sweet mother of all bottled bevvies. It was quite literally the mother of all alcopops as it was the alcoholic drink that started the whole hoo-har about drinks being advertised to underaged drinkers. It was a memory, or caused a lack of memory, of my misspent youth stood on street corners taking elicit sips and stashing the bottle when the plod drove by. I hadn't seen a bottle of Hooch in years. I didn't even know they still made it. Who would their market be? Teens of the noughties had long moved onto the more regular WKDs and

Smirnoff Ices. I have no idea what the alcopop of choice is today. When I saw the two bottles of Hooch in the chiller in the garage as I was picking up petrol, I just knew that I had to buy them for the evening's tipple.

Experiment number 4 – Can you open a bottle of alcohol with a belt?

Answer – not if you don't have a belt.

'So let me get this straight,' Harry began. 'We tried to light the kindling, which we ate, with a battery, that wouldn't work, to separate the fat out of the mayonnaise, which is low-fat, to fill the candle, which we don't have, while drinking bottles of booze, which we can't open.'

'That pretty much sums it up.'

'That's brilliant.' He beamed in the torchlight. After a moment's thought he continued. 'Jon, I've just had an idea. Rather than spending all that time making a candle, why don't we just use the massive flaming stove that is right in front of us.'

It wasn't a bad idea. And I did manage to get the bottles of Hooch open in the end by squeezing them in the handle of the mess tins. We toasted our ingenious experimentation and cleared up the mess we had made.

We clambered up the hill to the manicured lawn and threw our roll mats and bivvies out. I say throw because it quite literally is a throw. You pull the bivvy from its stuff sack, grip one end and launch the rest of it over the roll mat, just like you might make the beds at home.

I still love the ease at which setting out camp is achieved with a bivvy. Literally seconds after we had decided where to sleep and our beds were made. Where we had decided to sleep was bang in the middle of the manicured lawn. I have no idea how they were going to explain two rectangles of flattened grass in the middle of the lawn in the morning.

We snuggled in and stared up at the skies. This had been another night time microadventure and as we got nearer and nearer to the end of the Year of Microadventures we started reminiscing about the adventures gone past. I'd started writing this book so found it easy to recall each adventure we had been on whereas other than the biggies like the canoe trip and the birthday party on his farm, Harry struggled to remember the trips at all.

Maybe it was because he had so much else going on in his mad and manic life. Maybe it's because he doesn't have the repetitive nature that is being in a family. Maybe he just didn't look forward to the adventures in the same way that I did. Maybe it was just the fact that he hadn't had to go through them all again in his mind in preparation for writing a book about them. Whatever it was, it made me a little bit sad that he couldn't recall our time together. Each of those endless chats into the night while laying prone in a field or sitting around a campfire. Each of those misadventures where things hadn't gone as plan. Each of those epic challenges or journeys or exciting new things we'd done and he'd forgotten them.

Well bugger him, I thought. I'll have to write him an epic book that detailed each of our microadventures in full.

December

Just before I talk about the last one, I need to tell you about a man.

He is a very drunk man.

He is stumbling along the street after a works Christmas party.

Some of his friends fly by in a taxi shouting at him.

'Don't go and sleep in Epping Forest. Get in the cab and come and sleep on our floor.'

With a wave of his hand he ignores them and continues zig-zagging his way up the deserted street.

He walks for two hours.

He barely walks four miles.

He's never taken that long to walk that short a distance in his life.

He's very tired.

He can't walk any further.

He climbs a fence and collapses in a field.

Carefully I opened one eye to see if a throbbing migraine would start beating at the back of my eyeballs. It didn't.

I watched a flock of blackbirds take flight in the middle of field, silhouetted against the blues and oranges and reds of an early morning sunrise. To be fair, I don't know any sunrise that doesn't happen in the early morning. Also, to be honest, they could have been any other type of bird. In silhouette, all birds are black birds.

I raised my head off of my tiny travel pillow which somehow in my drunken state I had managed to remove from my bag and place under my head. I plucked the red and white Santa hat from my head and ruffled my itchy scalp. I was amazed that I appeared to be suffering from absolutely zero hangover. Something was clearly topsy turvy with the world. My legs burned with exhaustion but the rest of my physical being was fine.

A train rumbled past within metres of my prone body and brought me fully to consciousness.

I'd made my bed in what appeared to be a playing field for one of the local schools, not far from Loughton tube station. I'd not made it to Epping Forest, as I had promised myself all year that I would. I'd been about a mile short. However, falling asleep here did have its benefits as I swiftly stuffed my bivvy in my bag, strolled round the corner and almost instantaneously boarded a train that would take me in the direction of home.

Sleeping out after a night out is awesome, I've decided.

Harry and I were having real problems this month. We wanted to do something big but we were just both far too busy. I contacted Al to find out who in the area might be interested in meeting up for a mass microadventure. He got back to me to let me know that there was no formal group for North London but did point me towards some positive groups.

Harry also had loads of work commitments. Counter-intuitively the Christmas period is his busiest time as an ice-cream seller. He was getting tons of requests to flog his edible mist and liquid nitrogen ice cream concoctions at a whole host of corporate Christmas parties.

I on the other hand had both Rosie and Sally's birthdays, visits to see Santa, trips to the local pantomime to do and a whole heavenly host of other fun Christmas family activities to do.

I'm not saying I didn't want to do them. I did. I'd booked most of them myself. I love spending time with my family, especially when we're doing stuff together, rather than just sitting around the house watching TV.

What I had concerns about was that Harry and I were not going to fit our final microadventure of the year in.

After much toing and froing we found just one date when we were both free. It also happened to be the date that I'd arranged to meet up with Greg in that scum of South Wales city, Newport, Gwent. I'd promised him cinema tickets for his birthday.

Dum, dum, dum, dum-di-dum, dum-di-dum.

Yes, that's right! Star Wars 7 had come out and I'd booked three tickets. One for me. One for Greg. And one for Harry if he could make it.

Friday night and we raced along the M4 to Greg's house. Rosie insisted we listened to Frozen, on loop. She only relented when she requested (screamed) 'ROUND AND ROUND' from the back seat and Sally dully swapped the Disney CD for the nursery rhymes one.

We accelerated away from the Severn Bridge toll booth, beating all rival cars to the motorway, and sped into the crappiest city on earth, Newport, Gwent.

Greg opened his door and gave us each a massive hug. Harry was stood over his shoulder trying desperately NOT to look at Rosie. Ever since Harry had dropped an iPad on her when she was small, Rosie has never taken to Harry. Harry would probably not like me to mention that incident but I just find it funny. 'Rosie, were you dropped as a child?' 'No, I was hit by an iPad.' What a middle class dilemma!

Anyway, since that day, Rosie has screamed every time she sees Harry for the first time. Personally I think it is just that every time Harry sees Rosie he gets his big ugly four-eyed face up in her grill. He also tends to talk within the decibel range of a Harrier jump jet which is not always the best approach when first meeting small children. Or anybody come to think of it.

You could see the strain on Harry's face as he tried not to be as loud as a mating elephant. He was really struggling.

Dutifully I dragged all of the excess crap that comes with transporting toddlers around into the house and dumped it in the spare room. I made the cot, changed a nappy and heated the milk. Aren't I a good husband?

After making sure that Sally was A-OK, Greg, Harry and I bundled into Greg's Renault Picasso and bombed it across to the IMAX in Cardiff bay where we were due to watch the film.

Not just the film. THE film.

Most of the time I try to keep my inner geek in check but every now and again he breaks loose. I was going nerd-nuts. We were finally watching the film I had been waiting all year to see. Aaaaahh!

We (almost literally) skipped to the self-serve ticket machine as I had bought the tickets online. I put in my card and punched in my pin and three shiny tickets dropped out of the machine. I felt like Charlie on his way to the Chocolate Factory as I waved my golden (I wish it was golden) ticket.

The ticket said screen 13.

We looked around. There was no screen 13.

This wasn't looking good. I can't believe I've got a ticket for a screen that doesn't exist. For a split second I thought I wasn't going to get to see THE film. Then a kindly cinema employee pointed us toward the shiny glass lift in the middle of the foyer. It had a number 13 in massive illuminated letters over it. We got in and pushed a button.

Now I felt like Charlie in the Great Glass Elevator. My life had become a remake of Roald Dahl's children's books.

On the second floor Harry spied an unguarded fridge full of fizzy drinks and another one next to it full of tubs of popcorn. He glanced left and right and went for a bottle of 7up.

'You can't just take them Harry!' I whispered at him.

'I think you can,' he said. He shrugged his shoulders, split the seal on the drink and took a slug.

A large lady pushing a trolley walked up to us. Now we were in trouble.

'Take all you want lads. It's free,' she drawled in her Welsh accent.

What? Free popcorn and drinks! Where were we, Willy Wonka's Chocolate Room? I half expected to see a fountain of melted Cadbury's erupt from the floor.

We went around to the seating area where free nachos and dip were laid out on the tables. This was getting surreal. We gorged on popcorn and crisps and washed it down with coke and Fanta.

Soon a spotty lad called that the film was starting soon and we should take our seats. The three of us were the first at the doors and were led to our seats by a man with a small LED torch. He used it to gesture where our seats were. It looked like he was waving a tiny little lightsabre around, which just made us anticipate the oncoming film even more.

'Excuse me mate. I think you're in my seat.'

Wait, what?

I looked up at the big chap with the wide shoulders and the thick neck. A blonde lass tottered on high heels beside him and used his broad biceps as a crutch to save from breaking an ankle. I gulped back the any sort of response.

'Sorry sir,' said the lightsabre wielding cinema man. 'Can I have another look at your tickets, please?'

I passed mine across to him.

'Ah, these tickets are for yesterday.'

'Sorry, come again.'

'You see, because it's gone past midnight, it's now Saturday the 19th. Everyone here has the 19th on their ticket but yours says the 18th.'

'Ah, crap.' I looked at Harry and Greg. Both of them looked crestfallen. All this way, halfway across the country, to see a film I'd been waiting all year to see. And I'd booked the wrong bloody day. I was totally gutted.

'Don't worry,' said the torch man.

How could I not be worried?

'It happens all the time. We've got some spare seats further down. Please use them.'

Aha! We'd be seeing the film after all. We leapt out of our seats with joy and skipped down to our new allocation of seats further down the aisle.

In a better viewing location.

Win!

The film was good. Really good. But I'll let you go and see it and make your own mind up.

In an effort to keep Greg awake at three in the morning on the drive back, Harry and I started to play a game. It started innocently enough.

'How's your mum's dog been, Greg? I heard he was ill.'

'Yeah, Patch is doing much better, thanks. Especially since my dad has stopped smoking in the car with him.'

'Does he wear a nicotine *patch*?' asked Harry. So it begins.

'If he was a pirate, he'd wear and eye-*patch*.' I returned.

'That joke wasn't a *patch* on my one.'

'Do you know what's Greg's dog's favourite toy was when he was a puppy? The Cabbage *Patch* Kids.'

'When Greg's dog updates his computer he uses the most up-to-date *patch* available.'

'Greg's dog used to be a geography teacher. He had a blazer with *patch*es on the elbows.'

'Do you know Greg's dog's favourite film? *Patch* Adams!'

'Greg's dog has a really special blanket in his bed. It's a *patch*work quilt.'

YES! I'd won. Harry sat in silence pondering the various conjugations and meanings of the word 'Patch' while I marvelled at my own genius.

Like I said before, I'm really not that competitive.

So why have I told you a whole story about going to the cinema. Well there's a few reasons.

1) Harry and I had planned to have our last camp out of the year after the film had finished.
2) We didn't.
3) I didn't have much else to talk about for this month!

We'd planned to have our last camp out that night. However, I'd decided against it before I'd even left the house. I'd left all of my camping gear at home.

This time I'd said 'No'. I hadn't listened to my own advice about saying 'Yes' as much as possible. However, what I was doing is saying 'Yes' to something, or rather, someone else.

I'd decided that after all of this, after spending twelve months sleeping out under the stars, canoeing down remote rivers, gallivanting around coastal towns, trespassing on National Trust properties, completing an ultramarathon (ULTRAMARATHON!). After all of that the one thing I really wanted to do was spend a bit of time with my wife and child.

Throughout the whole year it had been a battle. Everything was about trying to squeeze adventure in at every corner, and it had been brilliant, inspiring and fun. I'd had the highs of waking up to a beautiful clear sky and the pleasant song of the dawn chorus and the lows of accidentally pooing my pants.

Through it all Sally had been at arms' length. She'd been giving me her blessing to go off and do daft stuff but she's been lamenting our precious time apart. She'd been selflessly giving me the green light while I self-indulgently went around the country pleasing myself and doing things just for me.

And even when I'd been doing stuff in the midweek, I'd been too knackered to be any use to anyone, man or beast, the following weekend. With our jobs, commuting and childcare complications we were both exhausted and the weekends were the only occasions that we could spend together.

I'd decided that the time had come to actually spend a bit of time with the woman I had chosen to spend the rest of my life with.

It had also been her (and Rosie's) birthday the week before.

So I booked a hotel in Cardiff for the following night and the three of us had a day just to ourselves before the mania of visiting family at Christmas began.

Other than the inevitable stress of last minute Christmas shopping, it was bliss just being together. Us three. Our little family.

That's not the end of it, though.

What I think I learnt from this Year of Microadventure wasn't the sleeping out, which never failed to make me feel good about myself (if a little bit drained the following few days). I liked the feeling of waking up with a fresh breeze on my face. I liked sharing my world with the wildlife. I liked the feeling of being up at 5am feeling like I was the only person on the planet. I loved being able to throw out my bivvy and be packed away in seconds in the morning. I loved the feeling of tranquility that comes with a camp out that is so often lost in this modern fast paced crazy mad place we live in today.

More than anything, I loved spending time with my mate. I loved the hours chatting about nothing in particular and the most important things in the world all at once.

What I learnt, though, was to prioritise. Sometimes it's great to chuck your backpack on your shoulder and just walk out the door. Sometimes it's even better to be snuggled at home with the ones you love. Either way, it's about making the most of your time on earth and reaching a balance. Every day, every hour, every minute, every second, every heartbeat is one step closer to the end.

When I get there I want to say that I've done something with my life.

Sounds a bit depressing but it's true. Life isn't a rehearsal. There are no reruns. You have one life so live it to the max. And that doesn't necessarily mean polar expeditions or trekking across the Sahara. It just means doing more now with your time. Be more creative. Be more adventurous. Get outside your comfort zone. Embrace the world. And spend time with those that mean the world to you. Because, when your world does end, the only place you will truly live on is in the memories of your loved ones. So make good memories together!

So this year I have pledged to find out what is important to me by finding a charity I can support. I've decided that I'm going to support and research 52 charities, one for each week of the year, and find out which one I like the best. Which one do I have the most connection with? Which one is worthwhile for my efforts and donations? Which one means something to me? Whichever one I choose, I will support that charity in everything else that I do until the day I die. I'll let you know what when I find out.

I've also decided to get outdoors more, but not just microadventures. I've decided to give it a purpose and I've persuaded Harry to join me, and my school to pay for me to complete a Mountain Leader course. Honestly, why the hell not? I spend enough time outdoors anyway.

I want to share the wonders of adventure with my family but at a pace that they will enjoy. I want to continue taking Sally out to the forest for walks through the trees. I want to continue going for hikes with Rosie and the baby carrier. And when it gets warmer, I want to take them both camping again. Let's see if I can get them bivvying by the end of the year! Baby steps first of all though.

Finally, when we're not adventuring I've come to the conclusion that I <u>need</u> to spend BETTER time with my wife and daughter. That means that when I am with them, I am completely with them. Not on my phone. Not watching TV (unless Sally wants to watch Silent Witness!). Just being there with them and enjoying my time with them.

And that is the reason that right now I am going to stop typing and go and give Sally a big kiss and thank her for putting up with me. Seeya!

If you are interested in doing your own microadventure, and I strongly encourage you do so (it's so easy!) then make sure you read Al's blog and, if you feel like it, buy his book which I massively recommend.

http://www.alastairhumphreys.com/

If you like the idea of Harry bringing one of his mad foodie machines to one of your corporate or social events then please book him. I've never used him, (apart from to stave of boredom, enrich my life, listen to my worst hang ups, etc. etc.) but I hear he is very good. Remember to ask for Charlie. And please don't call him up and abuse him down the phone. Only I'm allowed to do that!

http://www.lickmeimdelicious.com/

About the Author

Jon was a full time teacher who dreamed of adventure in his free periods. He has since jacked the teaching in to become a Stay at Home Dad (SAHD). His grandest adventure is probably failing to climb Mt. Kilimanjaro. He'd like to have a second stab one day. Jon likes to set himself stupid challenges. His current challenge is to attempt to do something different for 52 different charities in one year. He's not doing very well.

He also likes writing about himself in the third person.

Please feel free to follow him on Twitter @jondoolan1 or visit his website and blog jondoolan.com. He promises to be more media friendly in the future.

This is his first book and he hopes you enjoyed it. :)

Also by Jon Doolan

SARDINES

(The prequel to *Jon and Harry's Year of Microadventure*)

When Jon and his best mate, Harry, decided that they needed to inject some more fun activities into their lives they set out on a year-long challenge to complete 12 arbitrary missions set by a mysterious man from Facebook.

The Mission Challenger was born!

Buy it on Amazon NOW!

(Or later. Or whenever you feel like it. Or don't. It's completely up to you.)

jondoolan.com/sardines

Your honest feedback on *Jon and Harry's Year of Microadventure* would be massively appreciated:

https://www.facebook.com/jon.doolan
https://twitter.com/jondoolan1

Author, photographer, editor, proofreader, marketer, cover design, distributor and general nice guy: Jon Doolan. If it's crap, it's my fault.
Printing by CreateSpace

71973383R00082

Made in the USA
Columbia, SC
12 June 2017